TEMPTATION

Vaclav Havel

TEMPTATION

A play in ten scenes

*Translated from the Czech
by Marie Winn*

GROVE WEIDENFELD

New York

Pokouseni copyright © 1986 by Vaclav Havel
Published with permission of Rowohlt Verlag GmbH, Reinbek, Hamburg
Translation copyright © 1989 by Marie Winn

Published by Grove Weidenfeld
A division of Wheatland Corporation
841 Broadway
New York, NY 10003-4793

Library of Congress Cataloging-in-Publication Data

Havel, Vaclav.
  Temptation.

  Translation of: Pokouseni.
PG5039.18.A9P613 1989 891.8'625 88-13939

ISBN 0-8021-3100-X (pbk.)

Designed by Irving Perkins Associates

Manufactured in the United States of America

Printed on acid-free paper

First Edition 1989

3 5 7 9 8 6 4 2

For Zdenek Urbanek

TEMPTATION

CHARACTERS

Dr. Henry Foustka, scientist
Fistula, a retired cripple
Director
Vilma, a scientist
Deputy Director
Marketa, a secretary
Dr. Libushe Lorencova, a scientist
Dr. Vilem Kotrly, a scientist
Dr. Alois Neuwirth, a scientist
Mrs. Houbova, Foustka's landlady
Dancer
Petrushka
Secret Messenger
Lover (male)
Lover (female)

SCENES

The Institute
Foustka's apartment
The garden of the Institute
Vilma's apartment
The Institute

Intermission

Foustka's apartment
The Institute
Vilma's apartment
Foustka's apartment
The garden of the Institute

NOTE: *Before the curtain rises, during the pauses between scenes, and during the intermission, a particular piece of rock music of the "cosmic" or "astral" type may be heard. It is important that the pauses between scenes be as short as possible; consequently, the scene changes—in spite of various scenic requirements due to the alternating stage settings—should be carried out as swiftly as possible.*

Scene 1

One of the rooms of the scientific Institute where FOUSTKA is employed. It is something between a business office, a doctor's office, a library, a club room, and a lobby. There are three doors, one at the rear, one at the front left, one at the front right. At the right rear is a bench, a small table, and two chairs; against the rear wall is a bookcase, a narrow couch covered with oilcloth, and a white cabinet with glass windows containing various exhibits, such as embryos, models of human organs, cult objects of primitive tribes, etc. At the left is a desk with a typewriter and various papers on it, behind it is an office chair, and against the wall is a file cabinet; in the middle of the room hangs a large chandelier. There might be some additional equipment around, such as a sun lamp, a sink, or an exercise apparatus against the wall (specifically, a rypstol, a Swedish ladderlike gymnastic apparatus). The furnishings of the room are not an indication of any specific areas of interest or even of any particular personality but correspond, rather, to the indeterminate mission of the entire Institute. The combination of objects of various sorts and of various designs emphasizes the timeless anonymity of a space in which things have been brought together more by chance than for any definite purpose. As the curtain rises, LORENCOVA, KOTRLY, and NEUWIRTH are onstage. LORENCOVA, wearing a white doctor's coat, is seated at the desk, with a mirror propped up against the typewriter, where she is powdering her nose. KOTRLY, wearing a white coat, is sprawled out on the bench reading a newspaper. NEUWIRTH,

5

dressed in everyday clothing, is standing in the rear by the book-case, his back to the audience, looking at a book. There is a short pause.

LORENCOVA (*calling*): Marketa . . .

MARKETA (*wearing an office smock, enters through the door at left*): Yes, Doctor?

LORENCOVA: Would you please make me a cup of coffee?

MARKETA: Certainly.

KOTRLY (*without glancing up*): One for me too, please.

NEUWIRTH (*without turning around*): And me.

MARKETA: Will that be three, then?

LORENCOVA: Right.

(MARKETA *exits through the left door. A short pause, after which* FOUSTKA *enters quickly through the rear door, a bit out of breath. He is wearing black trousers and a black sweater and carries a briefcase.*)

FOUSTKA: Hi.

KOTRLY (*putting aside the newspaper*): Hello, Henry.

NEUWIRTH (*puts aside the book and turns around*): Hi.

(LORENCOVA *tucks the compact away in the pocket of her jacket and crosses the stage to the bench where* KOTRLY *is sitting, obviously making way at the desk for* FOUSTKA. *He sets his briefcase on it and hastily takes out some papers. The others watch him with interest.*)

FOUSTKA: Were they here yet?

KOTRLY: Not yet.

LORENCOVA: What's with Vilma?

FOUSTKA: She just ran across the street for some oranges.

(MARKETA *enters through the left door with three cups of coffee on a small tray. She puts two down on the table in front of* LOREN-COVA *and* KOTRLY, *the third she hands to* NEUWIRTH, *who is standing in the rear, leaning against the bookcase.*)

LORENCOVA: Thank you.

FOUSTKA: Marketa . . .

MARKETA (*stops*): Yes, Doctor?

FOUSTKA: I'm sorry, but could you possibly make one more cup for me?

MARKETA: Certainly.

FOUSTKA: Thanks a lot.

(MARKETA *exits through the left door.* LORENCOVA, KOTRLY, *and* NEUWIRTH *stir their coffees, at the same time watching* FOUSTKA, *who has seated himself at the desk and is straightening out various papers and files. Finally* KOTRLY *interrupts the rather long and somewhat tense silence.*)

KOTRLY (*to* FOUSTKA): So, what?

FOUSTKA: What, what?

KOTRLY: How's it going?

FOUSTKA: How's what going?

(LORENCOVA, KOTRLY, *and* NEUWIRTH *exchange glances and smile. A short pause.*)

LORENCOVA: Why, your private studies.

FOUSTKA: I don't know what studies you're talking about.

(LORENCOVA, KOTRLY, *and* NEUWIRTH *exchange glances and smile. A short pause.*)

NEUWIRTH: Come on, Henry, even the birds and bees in the trees are buzzing about it!

FOUSTKA: I'm not interested in what the birds and bees in the trees are buzzing about, and I have no other scholarly pursuits besides those directly concerned with my work at our Institute.

KOTRLY: You don't trust us, do you? I don't blame you. In certain situations caution is definitely in order.

NEUWIRTH: Especially if a person is playing both ends against the middle.

FOUSTKA (*quickly looks over at* NEUWIRTH): What do you mean by that?

(NEUWIRTH *moves his outstretched finger meaningfully around the room, pointing finally to the door at right, by which he means to indicate the powers that run the Institute, after which he points up and down, by which he means to indicate the power of heaven and hell.*)

You've all got overactive imaginations! Is the office party on tonight?

LORENCOVA: Of course.

(*The* DEPUTY DIRECTOR, *in everyday clothes, and* PETRUSHKA, *in a white coat, enter through the right door. They are holding hands, and will continue to hold hands during the entire play.*

This means that PETRUSHKA, *who doesn't speak a word during the entire play, usually follows the* DEPUTY DIRECTOR. *He, however, doesn't pay her any special attention, creating the impression, therefore, that he is dragging her around with him as some sort of prop or mascot.* LORENCOVA, KOTRLY, *and* FOUSTKA *stand up.*)

KOTRLY: Good morning, Sir.

DEPUTY: Hello there, my friends! And please sit down. You know that neither I nor the director like to stand on ceremony here.

(LORENCOVA, KOTRLY, *and* FOUSTKA *sit down again. A short pause.*)

So what's new. Did you all get a good night's sleep? Do you have any problems? I don't see Vilma here.

FOUSTKA: She called to say that her bus broke down. But apparently she managed to get a taxi and ought to be here very soon.

(*Short pause.*)

DEPUTY: Well, are you looking forward to the party? I hope you're all coming.

KOTRLY: I'm definitely coming.

LORENCOVA: We're all coming.

DEPUTY: Wonderful! I personally consider our office parties to be a marvelous thing—mainly for their collectively psychotherapeutic effect. Just think how quickly and easily those interpersonal problems that crop up among us from time to time are resolved in that informal atmosphere! And that's entirely due to the fact that as individuals we loosen up there somehow, while as a community we somehow tighten up. Isn't that the truth?

KOTRLY: That's precisely the way I feel about it.

DEPUTY: Apart from the fact that it would be an outright sin not to use such a beautiful garden at least once in a while! (*Pause.*) I came a little early on purpose . . .

NEUWIRTH: Did something happen?

DEPUTY: The director will tell you himself. Let me just ask you to be sensible, to try to understand him, and to try not to make his already rather difficult situation even more difficult unnecessarily. After all, we know we can't knock down walls with our heads, can we—why, then, should we complicate life for others and for our own selves! I think we can be glad we have the kind of director we have, so that by helping him we'll actually be helping our own selves. We should all bear in mind that essentially he's working for a good cause, that even he is not his own master, and that therefore we have no other alternative than to exercise at least that minimal amount of self-control necessary to make sure that neither he, our Institute, nor, consequently, any of us has any unnecessary problems. Actually there's nothing unusual about any of this. After all, a certain amount of inner discipline is required of everyone everywhere in today's world! I believe that you understand what I'm saying and that you won't expect me to tell you more than I can and have already told you. We're adults, after all, aren't we?

KOTRLY: Yes.

DEPUTY: So there you are! Have you received the soap allotment yet?

FOUSTKA: I'm going to distribute it today.

DEPUTY: Splendid!

(*The* DIRECTOR, *wearing a white coat, enters through the right door.* LORENCOVA, KOTRLY, *and* FOUSTKA *stand up immediately.*)

KOTRLY: Good morning, Sir.

DIRECTOR: Hello there, my friends! And please sit down. You know that I don't like to stand on ceremony here!

DEPUTY: That's precisely what I was telling our colleagues here just a second ago, Sir!

(LORENCOVA, KOTRLY, *and* FOUSTKA *sit down again. The* DIRECTOR *looks intently at those present for a while, then steps up to* FOUSTKA *and holds out his hand.* FOUSTKA, *surprised, rises.*)

DIRECTOR (*to* FOUSTKA): Did you get a good night's sleep?

FOUSTKA: Yes, thank you.

DIRECTOR: Do you have any problems?

FOUSTKA: Not really . . .

(*The* DIRECTOR *presses Foustka's elbow in a friendly way and turns to the others.* FOUSTKA *sits down again.*)

DIRECTOR: Where's Vilma?

DEPUTY: She called to say that her bus broke down. But apparently she managed to get a taxi and ought to be here very soon.

(MARKETA *enters through the left door with a cup of coffee. She hands it to* FOUSTKA.)

FOUSTKA: Thank you.

11

MARKETA: Don't mention it. (*Exits through the left door.*)

DIRECTOR: Well, are you looking forward to our party?

KOTRLY: Very much, Sir.

DEPUTY: Friends, I have some very good news for you on that subject: our director has promised to drop in for a moment tonight.

LORENCOVA: Just for a moment?

DIRECTOR: That will depend on the circumstances. (*To* FOUSTKA:) I hope you're coming.

FOUSTKA: Of course, Sir.

DIRECTOR: Look, colleagues, there's no sense in my dragging this out unnecessarily—we've all got enough work of our own. So, to get to the point: as you probably know by now, there have been an increasing number of complaints lately that our Institute is not fulfilling its mission in a way that responds to the present situation . . .

NEUWIRTH: What situation?

DIRECTOR: Let's not beat around the bush, my friend! Aren't you forgetting that we're supposed to be the first to hear about certain things and also the first to react to them? Isn't that what we're paid for! But that's not the problem. We're simply beginning to feel more and more pressure to start taking the offensive, meaning that through our widely publicized, popularized, pedagogical, cultural, scholarly, and individually therapeutic scientific work we must finally start confronting—

DEPUTY: In the spirit of scientific inquiry, of course . . .

DIRECTOR: Doesn't that go without saying?

12

DEPUTY: Excuse me, Sir, but there does exist, unfortunately, a certain science that is not based on the spirit of scientific inquiry.

DIRECTOR: That, in my opinion, is not a science! Where was I?

KOTRLY: You were saying that somehow we're supposed to finally start confronting . . .

DIRECTOR: Certain rather isolated but nonetheless alarming manifestations of those irrational attitudes cropping up primarily among a particular segment of the younger generation, and originating in an incorrect . . .

(*The* SECRET MESSENGER *enters through the right door, steps up to the* DIRECTOR, *and whispers at length into his ear. The* DIRECTOR *nods his head gravely as he whispers. After a long while the* MESSENGER *concludes. The* DIRECTOR *nods one more time. The* MESSENGER *exits through the right door. A short pause.*)

Where was I?

KOTRLY: You were saying that those irrational attitudes we're supposed to confront originate in an incorrect . . .

DIRECTOR: Understanding of the systemic complexity of natural phenomena and the historical dynamic of civilizational processes out of which certain incomplete aspects are extracted, only to be interpreted either in the spirit of pseudoscientific theory . . .

DEPUTY: We know for a fact that a number of illegal typescripts by C. G. Jung are circulating among the youth . . .

DIRECTOR: . . . or in the spirit of an entire spectrum of mystical prejudices, superstitions, obscure doctrines, and practices disseminated by certain charlatans, psychopaths, and intelligent people . . .

13

(VILMA, *out of breath, rushes in through the rear door, holding a bag of oranges.*)

VILMA: Please excuse me, Sir—I'm so sorry—but can you imagine that the bus I was riding—

DIRECTOR: I know about it, sit down . . .

(VILMA *sits on the oilcloth-covered couch, waves at* FOUSTKA, *and tries to communicate something to him via gestures and mime.*)

Look, colleagues, there's no sense in my dragging this out unnecessarily—we've all got enough work of our own. I've acquainted you with the basic facts of the situation, and our consequent duties, so now everything depends entirely on you. I would only like to ask you to be sensible, to try to understand me, and to try not to make my already rather difficult situation even more difficult unnecessarily. It's all for a good cause, after all! Aren't we living in a modern day and age, for heaven's sake?

KOTRLY: We are.

DIRECTOR: So there you are! Have you received the soap allotment yet?

FOUSTKA: I'm going to distribute it today.

(*The* DIRECTOR *steps up to* FOUSTKA; FOUSTKA *stands up. The* DIRECTOR *places his hand on his shoulder and gravely looks at him for a short while.*)

DIRECTOR (*gently*): I'm counting on you, Henry.

FOUSTKA: For the soap?

DIRECTOR: The soap and everything else!

The curtain falls.

14

Scene 2

Foustka's apartment. It is a smallish bachelor quarters with one door at the right rear. The walls are covered with bookshelves, which are filled with a great quantity of books. At the left is a window, in front of which is a desk covered with many papers and more books. Behind it is a chair. At the right is a low sofa. Beside it is a large globe. A star chart is hanging somewhere on the bookshelves. As the curtain rises, FOUSTKA, in a dressing gown, is kneeling in the middle of the room with four burning candles on the floor around him. He holds a fifth one in his left hand and a piece of chalk in his right hand, with which he draws a circle around himself and the four candles. A large old volume lies opened on the floor beside him. The room is dimly lit. When FOUSTKA completes his circle he glances at the book and studies something in it for a while. Then he shakes his head and mumbles something. At that moment someone knocks at the door. FOUSTKA is startled and jumps to his feet.

FOUSTKA (*calling out*): Just a minute!

(FOUSTKA *quickly turns on the light, blows out the candles, hastily puts them away somewhere behind his desk, puts away the volume, looks around, then with his foot tries to erase the chalk circle he had drawn on the floor.*)

(*calling:*) Who is it?

HOUBOVA (*offstage*): It's me, Professor.

FOUSTKA (*calling*): Come in, Mrs. Houbova.

HOUBOVA (*entering*): Boy, it's really smoky in here. You ought to air the place out.

FOUSTKA: I will, right away. Did something happpen?

15

HOUBOVA: You have a visitor.

FOUSTKA: Me? Who?

HOUBOVA: I don't know. He didn't introduce himself.

FOUSTKA: So it's someone you don't know.

HOUBOVA: He hasn't been here before—at least I've never seen him.

FOUSTKA: What does he look like?

HOUBOVA: Well—how can I put it—a little seedy—and mainly, well . . .

FOUSTKA: What?

HOUBOVA: It's embarrassing . . .

FOUSTKA: Just say it, Mrs. Houbova!

HOUBOVA: Well, he simply . . . smells . . .

FOUSTKA: Really? But how?

HOUBOVA: It's hard to describe . . . sort of like Limburger cheese . . .

FOUSTKA: My word! Well, never mind, show him in.

(HOUBOVA *exits, leaving the door ajar.*)

HOUBOVA (*offstage*): This way, please.

(FISTULA *enters. He is a smallish person, almost a dwarf, limping, and giving off a distinctly unsavory impression. He holds a paper bag containing his slippers.* HOUBOVA *casts a final glance after him, shrugs at* FOUSTKA, *and exits, closing the door behind her.* FISTULA *is grinning stupidly.* FOUSTKA *looks at him with surprise. A pause.*)

FOUSTKA: Good evening.

FISTULA: Greetings. (*Pause. Looks around him with interest.*) What a cozy place you have here, just as I'd imagined it. Good books—a rare globe—everything somehow as it ought to be—the balances don't lie.

FOUSTKA: I don't know what balances you're talking about. But first of all I don't even know who I'm speaking to . . .

FISTULA: All in good time. May I sit down?

FOUSTKA: Please.

(FISTULA *sits on the couch. Takes off his shoes, removes the slippers from the paper bag, puts them on, puts the shoes into the bag, and then places it on the sofa beside him. A pause.*)

FISTULA: I assume that I don't have to ask you not to mention my visit to anyone, for your sake as well as mine.

FOUSTKA: Why shouldn't I mention it?

FISTULA: You'll see why soon enough. My name is Fistula. Where I'm employed is of no importance, and in any event I don't even have a permanent position, nor do I need to have one, since I'm a cripple with a pension. (*Grins stupidly as if he has made a joke.*)

FOUSTKA: I'd guess that you work in a safety-match factory.

FISTULA (*chuckles, then suddenly grows serious*): That comes from a certain unidentified fungus of the foot. It makes me quite miserable and I do what I can for it, even though there's not much I can do.

(FOUSTKA *sits on the corner of the desk and looks at* FISTULA. *In his look we sense a mixture of curiosity, mistrust, and revulsion. A longer pause.*)

Aren't you going to ask me what I want or why I've come?

FOUSTKA: I'm ever hopeful that you'll tell me that yourself.

FISTULA: That, of course, would be quite possible, but I had a particular reason for not doing it until now.

FOUSTKA: What was it?

FISTULA: I was interested to see whether you'd figure it out for yourself.

FOUSTKA (*irately*): How could I figure it out when I've never seen you before in my life! In any case, I have neither the time nor the inclination to play guessing games with you. Unlike you, I happen to have a job and I'm leaving in a few minutes . . .

FISTULA: For the office party, right? But you've got heaps of time for that!

FOUSTKA: How do you know that I'm going to the office party?

FISTULA: And before my arrival you weren't exactly behaving like someone in a hurry either . . .

FOUSTKA: You don't know a thing about what I was doing before your arrival.

FISTULA: I beg your pardon, but I certainly know better than you do what I know and what I don't know, and how I know what I know!

(FISTULA *grins stupidly. A longer pause. Then* FOUSTKA *stands up, crosses to the other side of his desk, and turns gravely to* FISTULA.)

FOUSTKA: Look, Mister . . .

FISTULA: Fistula.

FOUSTKA: Look, Mister Fistula, I'm asking you plainly and

18

simply, in all seriousness, and I'm expecting a plain and simple, serious answer from you: What do you want?

(*A short pause.*)

FISTULA: Does the name Marbuel say anything to you? Or Loradiel? Or Lafiel?

(FOUSTKA *gives a start, quickly regains his control, gives a long shocked look at* FISTULA.)

FOUSTKA (*exclaiming*): Out!

FISTULA: Excuse me?

FOUSTKA: I said: Out!

FISTULA: What do you mean—out?

FOUSTKA: Leave my apartment immediately and never set foot in it again!

(FISTULA *rubs his hands contentedly.*)

Did you hear me?

FISTULA: I heard you clearly and I'm delighted by this reaction of yours because it absolutely confirms that I've come to the right place.

FOUSTKA: What do you mean?

FISTULA: Your fright, don't you see, makes it perfectly clear that you're fully aware of the importance of my contacts, which you wouldn't be if you hadn't been interested in the aforementioned powers earlier.

FOUSTKA: Those names don't mean a thing to me, I haven't the faintest idea of what you're talking about; moreover, the suddenness of my demand that you leave merely reflected the suddenness with which I became fed up with you. My

19

disgust coming at the same time that you pronounced those names was a complete coincidence! And now, having given you this explanation, I can only repeat what I said before, but this time without any fear that you might mistake my meaning: Leave my apartment immediately and never set foot in it again!

FISTULA: Your first request for me to leave—that I'll naturally grant, though probably not quite immediately. Your second request I will not grant, for which you will be very grateful to me later on.

FOUSTKA: You missed my meaning. Those weren't two independent requests, in fact they weren't requests at all. It was a demand—a single and indivisible one at that!

FISTULA: I'll make a note of it. But I'd also like to point something out: the haste with which you slipped in an additional motivation for your demand, together with the interesting fact that even though you claimed to be fed up with me, you considered it important enough to slip in this additional motivation even at the risk of delaying my longed-for departure—that haste together with that interesting fact are proof to me of one single thing: that your original fear of me as a middleman for certain contacts has now been superseded by a fear of me as a potential informer. Let me assure you, however, that I was counting on this phase as well. In fact had it not set in I would have felt quite uneasy. I would have considered it peculiar and would have wondered myself whether in fact *you* weren't an informer yourself. But now let me get down to business. There's obviously no way I can prove to you that I'm not an informer; even if I were to conjure up Ariel himself at this moment it still wouldn't eliminate the possibility of my being an informer. Therefore, you have only three choices.

First, to consider me an informer and to continue to insist on my immediate departure. Second, not to consider me an informer and to trust me. Third, not to make up your mind for the time being as to whether I'm an informer or not, but to adopt a waiting attitude, meaning on the one hand not to kick me out immediately and on the other hand not to say anything in front of me that might eventually be used against you if I actually *were* an informer. I'd like to recommend the third alternative.

(FOUSTKA *paces the room deep in thought; finally he sits down at his desk and looks over at* FISTULA.)

FOUSTKA: Very well, I'll accept that, but I'd like to point out that there's obviously no need for me to control or restrict my speech in any way because there's absolutely nothing I could possibly think, much less say, that might possibly be used against me.

FISTULA (*exclaiming*): Marvelous! (*Claps his hands with pleasure.*) You delight me! If I were an informer I'd have to admit that you avoided the first trap beautifully! Your declaration is clear evidence of your absolutely solid caution, intelligence, and quick wit, qualities that I eagerly welcome, since they give me hope that I'll be able to depend on you and that we'll be able to work together well.

(*Pause.*)

FOUSTKA: Listen, Mister . . .

FISTULA: Fistula.

FOUSTKA: Listen, Mister Fistula, I'd like to tell you two things. First of all, your talk is a bit redundant for my taste. You really ought to get to the point of what brought you here more quickly. You've said virtually nothing, even

21

though I asked you ages ago for a serious, direct, and concise answer to the question of what you actually want. And secondly, it surprises me greatly to hear that we're supposed to be working together on something. That requires two people, after all . . .

FISTULA: Your answer had eighty-six words. Considering its semantic value that isn't exactly a small number, and if I were you I wouldn't reproach anybody too severely for redundancy.

FOUSTKA: Bullshit is infectious, as we know.

FISTULA: I hope that as time goes by you'll adopt some of my more important skills as well.

FOUSTKA: You actually want to teach me something?

FISTULA: Not only to teach . . .

FOUSTKA: What else, for God's sake?

FISTULA (*crying out*): Leave him out of this!

FOUSTKA: Well, what else are you planning to do with me?

FISTULA (*smiling*): To initiate you . . .

(FOUSTKA *stands up abruptly and bangs his fist on the table.*)

FOUSTKA (*shouting*): That's enough! I'm a scientist with a scientific outlook on life, holding down a responsible job at one of our foremost scientific establishments! If anyone were to speak in my presence in a way that's obviously intended to spread superstition, I'd be forced to proceed in accordance with my scientific conscience!

(*For a moment* FISTULA *stares stupidly at* FOUSTKA, *then he suddenly begins to laugh wildly and dance around the room. Just as suddenly he falls silent, comes to a stop, stoops to the ground, and with his finger slowly traces the circle that* FOUSTKA *had drawn*

22

*there earlier, after which he jumps up and begins to laugh wildly
again. Then he goes over to the desk, seizes one of the hidden
candlesticks, waves it in the air and, still laughing, places it on
the desk.* FOUSTKA *watches him, goggle-eyed. Then suddenly,*
FISTULA *becomes serious again, returns to the couch, and sits
down.*)

FISTULA (*matter-of-factly*): I know your views well, Doctor
Foustka. I know how much you love your work at the
Institute, and I apologize for my foolish joke. Anyhow, it's
high time for me to cut out all this preliminary joking
around. As your director emphasized again this morning,
one of your Institute's tasks is to fight against certain manifestations of irrational mysticism that keep cropping up here
and there as a sort of obscurely preserved residue of the
prescientific thinking of primitive tribes and the Dark Ages
of history. As a scientist you know perfectly well that the
more thoroughly you're armed with knowledge about what
you're supposed to be fighting against, that much more
effective your fight will be. You have at your disposal quite a
decent collection of occult literature—almost all the basics
are here, from Agrippa and Nostradamus to Eliphas Levy
and Papus—nevertheless, theory isn't everything, and I
can't believe that you've never felt the need to acquaint
yourself with the practice of black magic directly. I come to
you as a sorcerer with several hundred successful magical
and theurgical evocations under his belt who is ready and
willing to acquaint you with certain aspects of this practice
in order to give you a base for your scientific studies. And in
case you're asking yourself why in the world a sorcerer
should want to join a battle against witchcraft, I can even
give you a convincing reply to that: I seem to be in a tricky
situation in which I might come to a bad end without cover
of some sort. I am therefore offering you my own self for
study, and I ask nothing in return besides your vouching for

23

me, if the need arises, that I turned myself over to the disposition of science, and that therefore it would be unfair to hold me responsible for the propagation of something which, in reality, I was helping to fight against.

(FISTULA *looks gravely at* FOUSTKA; FOUSTKA *reflects.*)

FOUSTKA (*quietly*): I have a suggestion.

FISTULA: I'm listening.

FOUSTKA: To expedite our communications I'm going to pretend that I'm not endowed with a scientific outlook and that I'm interested in certain things purely out of curiosity.

FISTULA: I accept your suggestion!

(FISTULA *steps up to* FOUSTKA *and offers him his hand;* FOUSTKA *hesitates a moment, then gives his hand to* FISTULA, *who clasps it.* FOUSTKA *instantly pulls his hand away in alarm.*)

FOUSTKA (*crying out*): Ow! (*Gasps with pain, rubs his hand and waves it in the air.*) Man, your temperature must be fifty below zero.

FISTULA (*laughing*): Not quite.

(FOUSTKA *finally recovers and resumes his seat at his desk.* FISTULA *also sits down, folds his hands in his lap, and stares with theatrically doglike resignation at* FOUSTKA. *A long pause.*)

FOUSTKA: So?

(*A long pause.*)

What's going on?

(*A long pause.*)

What's wrong with you. Have you lost your tongue all of a sudden?

24

FISTULA: I'm waiting.

FOUSTKA: For what?

FISTULA: For your command.

FOUSTKA: I don't understand: What command?

FISTULA: What better way for me to acquaint you with my work than for you to assign me certain tasks whose fulfillment you can verify for yourself and whose fulfillment matters to you for some reason?

FOUSTKA: Aha, I see. And what kind of tasks—roughly—should they be?

FISTULA: That's for you to say!

FOUSTKA: All right—but still and all—it's hard to think of anything under the circumstances . . .

FISTULA: Don't worry, I'll help you out. I think I have an idea for an innocent little beginning of sorts. If I'm not mistaken, there's a certain young lady you admire.

FOUSTKA: I don't know what you're talking about.

FISTULA: Doctor Foustka, after everything we've said here, you really must admit that I might occasionally know somebody's little secret.

FOUSTKA: If you're talking about the secretary of our Institute, I'm not denying that she's a pretty girl, but that doesn't necessarily mean . . .

FISTULA: What if tonight at the office party—quite unexpectedly and of course quite briefly—she were to fall in love with you? How about that?

(FOUSTKA *paces nervously for a short while, and then turns abruptly to* FISTULA.)

FOUSTKA: Please leave!

FISTULA: Me? Why?

FOUSTKA: I repeat—go away!

FISTULA: Are you beginning that again? I thought we'd reached an agreement.

FOUSTKA: You've insulted me.

FISTULA: How? In what way?

FOUSTKA: I'm not so badly off as to need magic for help in my love life! I'm neither a weakling incapable of manfully facing the facts when he doesn't manage to win by his own efforts, nor a cad who would carry out experiments on innocent and completely unsuspecting young girls for his own sensual pleasure. Do you take me for some sort of Bluebeard or what, Fistula?

FISTULA: Which of us knows what we really are! But that's not the issue now. If my well-intentioned, innocent, and quite spur-of-the-moment little idea touched a raw nerve for some reason, I naturally apologize and withdraw it!

FOUSTKA: And I didn't even mention my main objection: I'm involved in a serious relationship, and I'm faithful to my girl friend.

FISTULA: Just as faithful as she is to you?

FOUSTKA (*startled*): What do you mean by that?

FISTULA: Forget it.

FOUSTKA: Wait a minute, I'm not going to let you get away with making dirty insinuations like that! I'm not interested in gossip, and I don't like impudence!

26

FISTULA: I'm sorry I said anything. If you've decided to be blind, that's your business.

(FISTULA *removes his shoes from the paper bag and slowly begins to change footgear.* FOUSTKA *watches him uneasily. A pause.*)

FOUSTKA: You're leaving? (*Pause.*) I guess I blew up a little.

(*Pause.* FISTULA *has changed into his shoes, places his slippers in the bag, stands up, and slowly walks towards the door.*)

So what's going to happen?

FISTULA (*stops and turns around*): With what?

FOUSTKA: Well, with our agreement.

FISTULA: What about it?

FOUSTKA: Is it on?

FISTULA: That depends entirely on you. (*He grins.*)

The curtain falls.

Scene 3

The garden of the Institute. It is night, and the garden is illuminated by Chinese lanterns strung along wires attached to trees. In the middle of the stage is a small bower. Beyond it in the background is a space serving as a dance floor. In the front at the left is a garden bench; at the right is an outdoor table with a variety of bottles and glasses on it. All around are trees and bushes; these, together with the darkness, make it hard to see the dancing in the background as well as the various movements of figures in the garden. Only the action in the foreground is always clearly visible. As the curtain rises, the music grows softer and its character

27

changes; faintly audible now as if from a great distance are strains of popular dance music that will continue for the entire scene. The male and female LOVERS *are in the bower; they will remain there for the entire scene, gently embracing, caressing each other, kissing, and whispering into each other's ears, oblivious to the various goings-on around them. The* DEPUTY *with* PETRUSHKA, *and* KOTRLY *with* LORENCOVA, *are dancing as couples on the dance floor, while* VILMA *and the* DIRECTOR *are also there, each swaying separately to the music.* FOUSTKA *is standing at the table, pouring drinks into two glasses.* MARKETA *is sitting on the bench. Everyone is wearing evening clothes; the women wear long gowns. As the scene begins,* FOUSTKA *is explaining something to* MARKETA, *who is listening intently. As he is speaking* FOUSTKA *finishes pouring the drinks and slowly crosses over with them towards* MARKETA.*

FOUSTKA: We must realize that out of an infinity of possible speeds, the expanding universe chose precisely the one that would allow the universe itself to come into being as we know it, that is, having sufficient time and other requirements needed for the formation of solid bodies so that life would be able to begin on them—at least on one of them! Isn't that a remarkable coincidence!

MARKETA: That's really amazing!

(FOUSTKA *comes up to* MARKETA, *hands her a glass, sits down beside her, and both take a drink.*)

FOUSTKA: So there you are, and if you probe a bit further you'll discover that you owe your very existence to so unbelievable a multitude of similarly unbelievable coincidences that it exceeds the bounds of all probability. All those things can't exist just for themselves, can they? Don't they conceal some deeper design of existence, of the world, and of nature willing you to be you, and me to be me, willing life, simply, to exist, and at its very height, as we understand it for now,

28

the human soul, capable of fathoming it all! Or could it be, perhaps, that the cosmos directly intended that one fine day it would see itself thus through our eyes and ask itself thus through our lips the very questions we're asking ourselves here and now?

MARKETA: Yes, yes, that's exactly the way I see it!

(VILMA, *who has in the interim left the dance floor, now appears at the table and pours herself a drink.*)

VILMA: Are you enjoying yourselves?

FOUSTKA: Marketa and I are doing a bit of philosophizing.

VILMA: Well, I seem to be in the way here. (VILMA *disappears with her glass, and after a while she can again be seen dancing alone in the background. A pause.*)

FOUSTKA: And here's another thing. Modern biology has known for a long time that while the laws of survival and mutations and the like explain all sorts of things, they don't begin to explain the main thing: why does life actually exist in the first place, and above all why does it exist in that infinitely bright-colored multiplicity of its often quite self-serving manifestations, which almost seem to be here only because existence wants to demonstrate its own power through them? But to demonstrate to whom? To itself? Have you ever wondered about that?

MARKETA: To tell you the truth, no, not in this way . . . but from now on I'll probably think about it all the time. You know how to say things so nicely.

(NEUWIRTH *emerges from somewhere at the right. He steps up to the bench and bows to* MARKETA.)

NEUWIRTH: May I have the honor?

29

MARKETA (*in confusion*): Yes . . . of course.

(*She throws* FOUSTKA *a pleading, unhappy glance, and then rises.*)

FOUSTKA: You'll come back again, won't you?

MARKETA: Of course! Everything was so very interesting.

(NEUWIRTH *offers his arm to* MARKETA *and disappears with her. After a while they can be seen in the background dancing.* FOUSTKA *sips his drink, deep in thought. Shortly thereafter the* DIRECTOR, *who has in the interim left the dance floor, emerges from behind a bush at left, just in back of the bench.*)

DIRECTOR: A pleasant evening, isn't it?

(FOUSTKA *is a bit startled, and then quickly stands up.*)

FOUSTKA: Yes. We're in luck with the weather.

DIRECTOR: Please sit down. May I join you for a moment?

FOUSTKA: Of course.

(*They both sit down on the bench. An awkward pause. Then the* DIRECTOR *casually takes Foustka's hand and peers into his eyes.*)

DIRECTOR: Henry . . .

FOUSTKA: Yes?

DIRECTOR: What do you actually think of me?

FOUSTKA: I? Well . . . how shall I say it . . . I think that everyone in our Institute is glad that you're the one in charge . . .

DIRECTOR: You don't understand. I'm interested in what you yourself think of me—as a person—or, to be more precise, what you feel about me . . .

FOUSTKA: I respect you . . .

DIRECTOR: Is that all?

FOUSTKA: Well . . . how shall I say it . . . it's hard to . . . well, it's . . .

(*At that moment the* DEPUTY, *with* PETRUSHKA, *who have in the interim left the dance floor, appear at the right, holding hands. When the* DIRECTOR *sees them he drops Foustka's hand.* FOUSTKA *is obviously relieved.*)

DEPUTY: Here you are, Sir! We've been looking high and low for you.

DIRECTOR: Did something happen?

(*Making the most of the situation,* FOUSTKA *quietly stands up and quickly disappears.*)

DEPUTY: Nothing in particular. It's only that Petrushka here has a request to make of you, but she's just a little bashful about coming out with it . . .

DIRECTOR: What request?

DEPUTY: Whether she couldn't have a dance with you.

DIRECTOR: I don't know how to lead, and I'd only step all over her skirt. Really, there are so many better dancers here . . .

DEPUTY: In that case would you at least accept our invitation to come to the pool where our colleague Kotrly has constructed an adorable underwater light show.

(*The* DIRECTOR *peevishly gets to his feet and goes off somewhere to the right with the* DEPUTY *and* PETRUSHKA. *Just then* KOTRLY *and* LORENCOVA, *who have in the interim left the dance floor, appear at the left. They go to the table.*)

KOTRLY: Have you seen my underwater light show yet?

LORENCOVA: You're doing it stupidly, Willy.

KOTRLY: What am I doing stupidly?

(*They go up to the table and* KOTRLY *pours out two drinks and hands one to* LORENCOVA. *They sip their drinks.*)

LORENCOVA: You're being such an ass-kisser that even those two idiots will get sick of you. You'll end up a total joke and everybody will turn against you.

KOTRLY: Maybe I'm doing it stupidly, but it's still a lot better than pretending not to be interested, and all the while telling them everything!

LORENCOVA: Are you referring to Neuwirth?

KOTRLY: Who, for instance, was the first to begin talking about Foustka's interest in black magic? If they get wind of it, it'll be Neuwirth's doing!

LORENCOVA: But we all gossiped about it! You're being unfair to him and your only excuse is that you're jealous . . .

KOTRLY: It's just like you to stick up for him!

LORENCOVA: Are you beginning that again?

KOTRLY: Libby, give me your word of honor that you never had a thing with him!

LORENCOVA: Word of honor! Come on, let's dance!

(KOTRLY *and* LORENCOVA *put down their glasses on the table and exit somewhere off to the right. After a while they can be seen in the background, dancing. Meanwhile* NEUWIRTH *and* MARKETA *enter from the left.* MARKETA *sits down on the bench.* NEUWIRTH *hangs around nearby.* FOUSTKA *emerges from the bushes directly behind the bench and sits down next to* MARKETA. *An awkward pause.*)

NEUWIRTH: Oh dear, I seem to be in the way here.

(NEUWIRTH *vanishes. After a while he can be seen in the background, dancing with* LORENCOVA; *he has evidently cut in on* KOTRLY. *Meanwhile the* DEPUTY *and* PETRUSHKA *have appeared on the dance floor as well, dancing together, as well as the* DIRECTOR, *dancing alone again. A short pause.*)

MARKETA: Tell me more! Every word you say opens my eyes. I don't understand how I could have been so blind, so superficial . . .

FOUSTKA: I'll begin, if you don't mind, by taking a new tack. Has it ever occurred to you that we wouldn't be able to understand even the simplest moral action that doesn't serve some practical purpose? In fact, it would have to seem quite absurd to us if we didn't recognize that hidden somewhere in its deepest depths is the presumption of something higher, some sort of absolute, omniscient, and infinitely fair judge or moral authority through which and within which all our activities are somehow mysteriously appraised and validated and by means of which each one of us is constantly in touch with eternity?

MARKETA: Yes, yes, that's exactly how I've felt about it all my life! I just wasn't able to see it, let alone say it so beautifully.

FOUSTKA: So there you are! What's even more tragic is that modern man has repressed everything that might allow him somehow to transcend himself, and he ridicules the very idea that something above him might even exist and that his life and the world might have a higher meaning of some sort! He has crowned himself as the highest authority, so he can then observe with horror how the world is going to the dogs under that authority!

MARKETA: How clear and simple it is! I admire the way you're able to think about everything so . . . so, well, in your own way somehow, differently from the way most people usually

33

talk about it, and how deeply you feel all those things! I don't think I'll ever forget this evening! I have a feeling that I'm becoming a new person every minute I'm with you. Please forgive me for saying it so openly, but it's as if something were radiating from inside of you that—I don't understand how I could have walked by you so indifferently before—it's simply that I've never felt anything like this before . . .

(KOTRLY *emerges from somewhere at the right, goes up to the bench, and bows to* MARKETA.)

KOTRLY: May I have the honor?

MARKETA: I'm sorry, but I . . .

KOTRLY: Come on, Marketa, we haven't had a single dance together!

(MARKETA *looks unhappily at* FOUSTKA, *who just shrugs his shoulders helplessly;* MARKETA *stands up.*)

MARKETA (*to* FOUSTKA): You'll wait here, won't you?

FOUSTKA: Of course I'll wait.

(KOTRLY *offers an arm to* MARKETA *and disappears with her. After a while they may be seen in the background, dancing.* FOUSTKA *sips his drink, deep in thought. After a short while the* DIRECTOR, *who has in the interim left the dance floor, emerges from behind a bush directly in back of the bench.*)

DIRECTOR: Alone again?

(FOUSTKA *is a bit startled, then quickly stands up.*)

Sit down, Henry.

(FOUSTKA *sits again. The* DIRECTOR *sits down beside him. A short pause.*)

Do you smell that wonderful fragrance? Acacias . . . nasturtiums . . .

FOUSTKA: I don't know very much about fragrances.

(*An awkward pause. Then the* DIRECTOR *again casually takes Foustka's hand and gazes closely into his eyes.*)

DIRECTOR: Henry . . .

FOUSTKA: Yes?

DIRECTOR: Would you like to be my deputy?

FOUSTKA: Me?

DIRECTOR: I could arrange it.

FOUSTKA: But you already have a deputy.

DIRECTOR: If you only knew what a pain in the ass he gives me!

(*Just then the* SECRET MESSENGER *enters, goes up to the* DIRECTOR, *leans over, and whispers at length into his ear. The* DIRECTOR *gravely nods his head. After a longer time the* MESSENGER *concludes. The* DIRECTOR *nods one more time. The* MESSENGER *exits to the right. The* DIRECTOR, *who had not dropped Foustka's hand during the whispering, turns again to* FOUSTKA *and gazes closely into his eyes for a longer time.*)

Henry.

FOUSTKA: Yes?

DIRECTOR: Wouldn't you like to stop over at my place for a little while after the party? Or if you don't want to stay to the end, we could both slip away without anyone noticing. I've got some homemade cherry liqueur. I could show you my collection of miniatures, we could chat in peace and quiet, and if we happened to go on too long and you didn't feel like going home that late, you could easily spend the night at my place! You know that I live all alone, and what's more, it's only a hop and a skip from our Institute, so you'd have it that much easier in the morning—what do you say?

FOUSTKA: I'm very honored by your invitation, Sir, but I'm afraid I've already promised that I'd go to . . .

DIRECTOR: To Vilma's?

(FOUSTKA *nods. The* DIRECTOR *gazes closely into his eyes for another moment, then, all at once, drops his hand briskly, stands up abruptly, crosses over to the table, pours himself a drink, and quickly drains it.* FOUSTKA *remains seated on the bench, embarrassed. Then the* DEPUTY, *with* PETRUSHKA, *who have in the interim left the dance floor, emerge from the left, holding hands.*)

DEPUTY: Here you are! We've been looking all over . . .

DIRECTOR: Did something happen?

DEPUTY: Nothing in particular. Me and Petrushka here, we just wanted to ask you if you had any plans after the party. We'd consider it quite an honor if you'd accept our invitation to come over for a little nightcap before bedtime. You could even spend the night at our house—if you wanted to, of course . . .

DIRECTOR: I'm tired and I have to go home. Goodbye.

(*The* DIRECTOR *exits quickly to the right. The* DEPUTY *looks after him in confusion, then, somewhat crestfallen, disappears with* PETRUSHKA *to the left. After a while they may be seen in the background, dancing. Just then* NEUWIRTH *and* LORENCOVA, *who have in the interim left the dance floor, appear near the table at the right.*)

NEUWIRTH: I've seen a lot of things in my day, but an educated

36

person sucking up to his idiot bosses with ridiculous stunts like those light bulbs in the pool—that really takes the cake! (*He pours two drinks, hands one to* LORENCOVA; *they both sip.*)

LORENCOVA: Sucking up with the light bulbs is still a lot better than pretending not to be interested and all the while telling them everything!

NEUWIRTH: It's just like you to stick up for him!

LORENCOVA: Are you beginning that again?

NEUWIRTH: Libby, give me your word of honor that you never had a thing with him!

LORENCOVA: Word of honor! Come on, let's dance!

(NEUWIRTH *and* LORENCOVA *put their glasses down on the table and exit somewhere to the left. After a while they can be seen in the background, dancing. Meanwhile* KOTRLY *and* MARKETA *enter from the right.* MARKETA *sits down on the bench next to* FOUSTKA. KOTRLY *hangs around nearby. An awkward pause.*)

KOTRLY: Oh dear, I seem to be in the way here.

(KOTRLY *vanishes. After a while he can be seen in the background, dancing with* LORENCOVA. *He has evidently cut in on* NEU-WIRTH.)

FOUSTKA: When a person casts God from his heart, he opens a door for the devil. When you think about the increasingly stupid willfulness of the powerful and the increasingly stupid submission of the powerless, and the awful destruction committed in today's world in the name of science—and after all we *are* its somewhat grotesque standard-bearers—isn't all that truly the work of the devil? We know that the devil is a master of disguises, and what more ingenious

37

disguise could one imagine than the one offered him by the godlessness of modern times? Why, he must find the most promising base of operations in those very places where people have stopped believing in him! Please forgive me for speaking so openly, Marketa, but I can't keep it stifled inside me any longer! And who else can I confide in besides you?

(MARKETA *throws her glass into the bushes and grasps Foustka's hand emotionally.*)

MARKETA (*exclaiming*): I love you!

FOUSTKA: No!

MARKETA: Yes, I'll love you forever!

FOUSTKA: Oh, you poor creature! I'd be your ruin!

MARKETA: I'd rather be ruined with you and live the truth than be without you and live a lie!

(MARKETA *embraces* FOUSTKA *and begins to kiss him passionately. Just then* VILMA, *who has in the interim left the dance floor, appears at the table. For a moment she observes the embracing couple.*)

VILMA (*icily*): Are you enjoying yourselves?

(FOUSTKA *and* MARKETA *immediately pull apart and look at* VILMA *in a state of shock.*)

The curtain falls.

Scene 4

Vilma's apartment. It is a cozy boudoir, furnished with antiques. There is a door at the rear. At the left is a large bed with a canopy.

At the right are two small armchairs, a large Venetian mirror, and a vanity table with a large collection of perfumes on it. Scattered about the room are various female odds and ends and trinkets. The only thing folded neatly is Foustka's evening outfit next to the bed. The colors are all feminine, predominantly pink and purple. As the curtain rises, FOUSTKA is sitting in his undershorts at the edge of the bed, and VILMA, in a lacy slip, is sitting at the vanity table combing her hair, facing the mirror with her back to FOUSTKA. A short pause.

FOUSTKA: When was he here last?

VILMA: Who?

FOUSTKA: Stop asking stupid questions!

VILMA: You mean that dancer? About a week ago.

FOUSTKA: Did you let him in?

VILMA: He just brought me some violets. I told him I had no time, that I was hurrying to meet you.

FOUSTKA: I asked you whether you let him in.

VILMA: I don't remember anymore . . . maybe he came in for a moment.

FOUSTKA: So you kissed him!

VILMA: I kissed him on the cheek to thank him for the violets, that's all.

FOUSTKA: Vilma, don't treat me like a fool, for goodness sake! I just bet you could buy him off with a mere kiss on the cheek once you let him in! Surely he tried to dance with you at the very least.

VILMA: Henry, drop it, for goodness sake! Can't you talk about anything more interesting?

FOUSTKA: Did he try or not?

VILMA: All right, he did, if you really must know! But I won't tell you another thing! I simply refuse to keep talking to you on this level, because it's embarrassing, undignified, insulting, and ridiculous! You know very well that I love you, and that no dancer could possibly be a threat to you, so stop tormenting yourself with this endless cross-examination! I don't keep pumping you for details either—and I'd have far more reason to do so!

FOUSTKA: So you refuse to tell? Well in that case everything is quite clear.

VILMA: But I've told you a hundred times that I don't go out of my way to see him, I don't care for him, I don't dance with him, so what else am I supposed to do, damn it!

FOUSTKA: He hangs around you, he flatters you, he wants to dance with you all the time—and you enjoy it! If you didn't enjoy it, you'd have gotten rid of him long ago.

VILMA: I won't deny that I enjoy it—any woman would enjoy it. His persistence is touching, and so is the very fact that he never gives up, even though he knows perfectly well that he doesn't have a chance. Would you, for instance, be capable of driving here at night from God knows where for no other reason than to bring me some violets, even though you knew the situation was hopeless?

FOUSTKA: He's persistent because you deliberately dash his hopes in a way that keeps them alive and you deliberately reject him in a way that makes him long for you more and more! If you really slammed the door on his hopes he'd never show up here again. But you wouldn't do that, because it amuses you to play cat and mouse with him. You're a whore!

40

VILMA: You've decided to insult me?

FOUSTKA: How long did you dance together?

VILMA: Enough, Henry, you're beginning to be disgusting! I've always known that you're eccentric, but I really never suspected that you're capable of being this nasty! What's suddenly brought on this pathological jealousy of yours? This insensitivity, tactlessness, maliciousness, vengefulness? At least if you had any objective reason for it . . .

FOUSTKA: So you're planning to keep whoring around?

VILMA: You have no right to talk to me like that! You kept pawing at that girl all evening, everybody's embarrassed, I wander around like an idiot—people feel sorry for me all over the place—and now you have the nerve to reproach me! Me! You do as you damn well please, I just have to suffer in silence, and finally you make a scene here on account of some crazy dancer! Do you see how absurd it is? Do you realize how terribly unfair it is? Do you have the faintest idea of how selfish and cruel you are?

FOUSTKA: In the first place, I was certainly not pawing anyone and I'd like you to please refrain from using words like that, especially when you're referring to pure creatures like Marketa. In the second place, we're not discussing me, but you, so kindly stop changing the subject. Sometimes I get a feeling that there's some monstrous plan hidden behind all this. First, you'll resurrect feelings within me that I'd assumed were dead long ago, and then once you've deprived me thus of my well-known objectivity, you'll begin to tighten a web of deceit around my heart, lightly at first, but then ever more painfully, an especially treacherous one because it is composed of a multitude of delicate threads of dancerly pseudoinnocence! But I won't let myself be

41

tortured on this rack any longer! I'll do something either to myself—or to him—or to you—or to all of us!

(VILMA *puts down her comb, begins to clap her hands, and walks towards* FOUSTKA *with a smile.* FOUSTKA *also begins to smile, stands up, and walks towards* VILMA.)

VILMA: You keep getting better and better!

FOUSTKA: You weren't bad yourself.

(FOUSTKA *and* VILMA *gently embrace, kiss, and then slowly get into bed together. They settle down together comfortably, lean back against the pillows, and cover their legs with a blanket.* FOUSTKA *lights a cigarette for himself and for* VILMA. VILMA *finally ends a long pause by speaking.*)

VILMA: Henry.

FOUSTKA: Hmm . . .

VILMA: Isn't it beginning to get on your nerves just a bit?

FOUSTKA: What?

VILMA: You know, that I keep making you play these games.

FOUSTKA: It did bother me for quite a long time.

VILMA: And now?

FOUSTKA: Now just the opposite—it's beginning to scare me.

VILMA: To scare you? Why?

FOUSTKA: I have a feeling that I'm beginning to get into it too much.

VILMA (*exclaiming*): Henry! Don't tell me you're really beginning to get jealous! Now that's fantastic! Never in my wildest dreams did I hope it would succeed like this! I had

42

become resigned to the idea that you'd never feel any jealousy other than the make-believe kind.

FOUSTKA: I'm sorry, but I can't share your delight.

VILMA: I don't understand what you're afraid of!

FOUSTKA: My own self!

VILMA: Come on!

FOUSTKA: Don't underestimate it, Vilma. Something's happening to me. I suddenly feel capable of doing all sorts of things that have always been alien to me. It's as if something dark inside of me were suddenly beginning to flow out of its hiding place and into the open.

VILMA: What an alarmist you are! You're beginning to feel a little healthy jealousy and that throws you into a complete panic! There's nothing wrong with you. Maybe you're just a little upset because your situation at the Institute came to a head this evening with that unfortunate incident with the director. That's obviously on your mind, and it's working away at your unconscious, looking for some way out, even though you won't admit it. That's why you're beginning to see bogeymen all over the place.

FOUSTKA: If only it were that simple.

(*Pause.*)

VILMA: Do you think he'll destroy you?

FOUSTKA: He'll certainly try. The question is whether he has enough power to do it.

VILMA: But he's got all the power he wants—all the power there is, actually—at least as far as we're concerned.

FOUSTKA: There are other kinds of power besides the kind he dispenses.

43

(VILMA, *horrified, jumps up and kneels on the pillow opposite* FOUSTKA.)

VILMA: Do you mean that seriously?

FOUSTKA: Hmm . . .

VILMA: Now you're scaring me! Promise me you won't dabble in that sort of thing!

FOUSTKA: And what if I won't promise?

VILMA: The minute you mentioned that cripple I knew there'd be hell to pay! He's addled your brains! You'd actually go so far as to get involved with him?

FOUSTKA: Why not?

VILMA: This is horrible!

FOUSTKA: At least you see that I wasn't just kidding around before.

(*Just then the doorbell rings.* VILMA *cries out in horror and quickly huddles up under the blankets.* FOUSTKA *smiles, calmly gets out of bed, and dressed just as he is—that is, in his undershorts—goes to the door and quickly opens it. There stands the* DANCER *holding a bunch of violets behind his back.*)

DANCER: Good evening. Is Vilma home?

FOUSTKA: Why?

DANCER (*points to the flowers*): I just wanted to give her a little something.

FOUSTKA (*calling to the bed*): Vilma, you have a visitor.

(VILMA *climbs out of bed, is a bit confused, can't quickly find anything to cover up with, and therefore goes to the door dressed only in her slip.* FOUSTKA *steps to the side, but does not go away.*)

VILMA (*to the dancer, with embarrassment*): Is that you?

DANCER: I'm sorry to disturb you at this hour—we were on tour—I just wanted to give you—here.

(*The* DANCER *hands* VILMA *the violets,* VILMA *takes them and sniffs them.*)

VILMA: Thank you.

DANCER: Well, I'll be going again. I apologize again for disturbing you.

VILMA: Bye-bye.

(*The* DANCER *exits.* VILMA *closes the door, smiles uncertainly at* FOUSTKA, *puts down the violets somewhere, steps up to him, embraces him, and gently kisses his forehead, lips, and cheek.* FOUSTKA *stands motionless and looks coldly in front of him.*)

I love you.

(FOUSTKA *doesn't move a hair.* VILMA *continues to kiss him. Then, suddenly,* FOUSTKA *slaps her brutally in the face.* VILMA *falls to the ground.* FOUSTKA *kicks her.*)

The curtain falls.

Scene 5

The same room at the Institute as in Scene 1. As the curtain rises, nobody is onstage, but very soon VILMA *and* FOUSTKA *enter through the rear door.* FOUSTKA *is wearing the same evening clothes he wore at the party the previous day.* VILMA *is wearing a white coat. She has a black eye. They both seem happy.*

VILMA: We can't be the first!

FOUSTKA: Have you noticed that you come to work on time only when I stay over at your place?

VILMA: You're exaggerating.

(FOUSTKA *sits down at the desk and begins to sort out some papers.* VILMA *sits down on the oilcloth couch.*)

(*Calling.*) Marketa.

(MARKETA, *wearing an office smock, enters through the left door. When she sees* FOUSTKA *she stops abruptly and lowers her eyes.*)

Would you please make us two cups of coffee? A bit stronger, if possible.

MARKETA: Yes, of course.

(MARKETA *goes a bit nervously towards the left door, stealthily glancing over at* FOUSTKA, *who looks up from his papers and smiles at her jovially.*)

FOUSTKA: Well, did you get a good night's sleep?

MARKETA (*stuttering*): Thank you—yes—actually no. There were so many thoughts racing through my head. (MAR-KETA, *in some confusion, exits through the left door.*)

VILMA: I think you turned that poor little thing's head last night.

FOUSTKA: Oh, she'll get over it.

(*Pause.*)

VILMA: Henry.

FOUSTKA: Yes, darling?

VILMA: It hasn't been that good in a long time, has it?

FOUSTKA: Hmm . . .

46

(LORENCOVA *in a dress,* KOTRLY *also in civilian clothes, and* NEUWIRTH *in a white coat enter through the rear door.*)

KOTRLY: You're here already?

VILMA: Hard to believe, isn't it?

(LORENCOVA *and* KOTRLY *sit down at their places on the bench;* NEUWIRTH *leans against the bookcase.*)

LORENCOVA (*looks at Vilma's face*): My God, what's that?

VILMA: Oh you know, deathless passion.

(MARKETA *enters through the left door with two cups of coffee on a tray. She hands one to* VILMA, *and sets down the other with somewhat trembling hands in front of* FOUSTKA.)

FOUSTKA: Thanks.

LORENCOVA: Some for us too, Marketa.

MARKETA: Yes, Doctor Lorencova.

(MARKETA *exits quickly through the left door. The* DEPUTY, *in a white coat, and* PETRUSHKA, *in a dress, enter through the right door. They are holding hands. Everyone stands.*)

KOTRLY: Good morning, Sir.

DEPUTY: Hello there, my friends! I see we've got perfect attendance here today—that's fantastic—today of all days I would have least expected it. (*Everyone sits down again.*) I think that yesterday was a real success. You all deserve thanks for that. But I must express special appreciation to our colleague Kotrly here for his underwater light effects.

KOTRLY: Please don't mention it.

DEPUTY: Well, my friends, there's no point in beating around the bush any longer.

NEUWIRTH: Did something happen?

DEPUTY: The director will tell you himself. At this time I just want to implore you all to understand that certain things have to be the way they are, to meet us halfway as we meet you halfway, and, mainly, to keep a cool head, a glowing heart, and clean hands at this crucial point in time. In short, there are times when people either come through with flying colors, and then they have nothing to fear, or they don't come through, and then they have only themselves to blame for the unnecessary troubles they create as a result. But you're educated people, after all—I don't have to spell it all out for you. Who'll volunteer for garden cleanup?

KOTRLY: I might as well, after all I have to go there anyhow to terminate the light bulbs.

DEPUTY: Splendid!

(*The* DIRECTOR, *in civilian clothes, enters through the right door. Everyone stands again.*)

KOTRLY: Good morning, Sir.

DIRECTOR: Hello there, my friends! I see we've got perfect attendance here today—that's fantastic—today of all days I would have least expected it and today of all days it's especially important.

DEPUTY: That's precisely what I was telling our colleagues just a second ago, Sir.

(*Everyone sits again. The* DIRECTOR *looks intently at those present for a moment and then steps up to* KOTRLY *and shakes his hand.* KOTRLY *stands up, surprised.*)

DIRECTOR: Did you get a good night's sleep?

KOTRLY: Yes, thank you.

DIRECTOR: Do you have any problems?

KOTRLY: Not really.

(*The* DIRECTOR *presses Kotrly's elbow in a friendly way and turns again to the others.* KOTRLY *sits again.*)

DIRECTOR: There's no point in beating around the bush, friends . . .

NEUWIRTH: Did something happen?

DIRECTOR: As we know, our Institute is a kind of lighthouse of truthful knowledge. I'd even go so far as to say it's something of a faithful watchdog over the scientific core of science itself—it's something like the avant-garde of progress. Therefore one might simplify it thus: We think it today, they'll live it tomorrow!

DEPUTY: I've already reminded our colleagues, Sir, of the responsibility that our mission involves.

DIRECTOR: But here's why I'm saying all this: a serious thing has happened . . .

(*Just then the* SECRET MESSENGER *enters through the right door, steps up to the* DIRECTOR, *and whispers at length into his ear. The* DIRECTOR *gravely nods his head. After a long while the* MESSENGER *concludes. The* DIRECTOR *nods one more time and continues speaking. The* MESSENGER *exits through the right door.*)

But here's why I'm saying all this: a serious thing has happened . . .

(*Just then* MARKETA *enters through the left door carrying a tray with three cups of coffee on it. She places two on the table in front of* LORENCOVA *and* KOTRLY *and hands the third to* NEUWIRTH. *Then she heads back towards the left door.*)

But here's why I'm saying all this: a serious thing has happened . . .

(MARKETA *stops in her tracks, glances at the* DIRECTOR *and at* FOUSTKA, *then she quietly goes up to the left door and eavesdrops.*)

NEUWIRTH: Did something happen?

DEPUTY (*to* NEUWIRTH): Please stop interrupting the director! Didn't you hear him say that he's about to tell you . . .

DIRECTOR: A serious thing has happened: a virus has lodged itself where one would have least expected it, yet in the very place it can do the worst damage—that is, in the very center of antiviral battle—indeed, if I'm to stick with this metaphor, right in the central antibiotic warehouse!

(*Everyone looks at each other anxiously.* VILMA *and* FOUSTKA *exchange a glance that reveals they know there's trouble ahead.* FOUSTKA *nervously gropes for a cigarette and lights up.*)

KOTRLY: Are you saying, Sir, that right here, among us, there's someone . . .

DIRECTOR: Yes, with deep sorrow, bitterness, and shame I must say precisely that. We have a scientific worker here at this Institute—let me emphasize the word *scientific*—who has long and of course secretly, which only confirms his two-faced nature, been involved with various so-called occult disciplines, from astrology through alchemy all the way to black magic and theurgy, in order to probe those murky waters for a would-be hidden wealth of an allegedly higher—that is prescientific—kind of learning.

KOTRLY: You mean he believes in spirits?

DIRECTOR: Not only that, but he is actually attempting to move from theory to practice! We have ascertained that he has established contact—

LORENCOVA: With spirits?

DEPUTY: He'd have a bit of trouble doing that, wouldn't he, Sir?

DIRECTOR: That's enough! Please don't joke about things that leave a black mark on the work of our Institute, things that are a direct assault on its reputation and therefore a low blow to us all, and especially to me as the one responsible for all of its scientific credibility. It is a grave and sad matter, my friends, and it's up to all of us to come to grips with it honorably! Where was I?

DEPUTY: You were discussing those contacts . . .

DIRECTOR: Ah yes. Well, then, we have learned that not long ago he established direct contact with a certain element from that no-man's-land of pseudoscience, common criminality, and moral turpitude, who is suspect not only because he spreads superstition and deludes the credulous by means of various tricks, but who actually dabbles in Satanism, black magic, and other such poisonous practices. That's the fact of the matter, and now I'd like to open this up for discussion. Does anyone have any questions?

(*An oppressive pause.*)

KOTRLY (*quietly*): Might I ask the name of this colleague?

DIRECTOR (*to the* DEPUTY): Say it!

DEPUTY: I can hardly utter the words, but name him I must. We're talking about Doctor Foustka, here.

(*An oppressive pause.*)

DIRECTOR: Who else wishes to speak?

MARKETA (*timidly*): I do.

FOUSTKA (*quietly to* MARKETA): Please, I beg of you, stay out of this!

51

DIRECTOR: This concerns us all. Even the secretary here deserves a chance to speak her mind.

MARKETA: Please excuse me, Sir. I'm not a scientist and I don't know how to express myself too well, but that simply can't be true! Doctor Foustka is a wise and honorable man—I know he is—he worries about questions that we really all should be worrying about—he thinks for himself—he tries to get to the bottom of the deepest questions—the source of morality—of universal order—and all those other things—and those contacts you mentioned—I simply don't believe it! Surely these are all wicked lies spread by bad people who want to harm him.

(*A deathly silence falls over the room.* FOUSTKA *is obviously in despair over Marketa's outburst. After a while the* DIRECTOR *turns matter-of-factly to the* DEPUTY.)

DIRECTOR (*to the* DEPUTY): As soon as we're finished, please arrange for her immediate dismissal! Now of all times our Institute truly can't allow itself the luxury of employing a secretary who accuses the administration of lying!

DEPUTY: I'll take care of it, Sir.

DIRECTOR (*to* MARKETA): You may go get your things together.

FOUSTKA (*in a muffled voice to* MARKETA): You've gone mad—to ruin your life so foolishly like this—why, you won't get a job anywhere!

MARKETA: I want to suffer with you!

FOUSTKA: Excuse me, Sir, but wouldn't it be more sensible to have her hospitalized? It's perfectly obvious that she doesn't know what she's saying.

52

DIRECTOR: Psychiatry, Doctor Foustka, is not a garbage dump for girls you've used and thrown away.

MARKETA: Henry, are you renouncing me? And everything you told me last night, are you renouncing that too?

FOUSTKA (*speaking furiously through clenched teeth*): For God's sake, keep quiet!

(MARKETA *bursts into tears and runs out the left door. An awkward pause.*)

VILMA (*quietly to* FOUSTKA): If she does something rash it'll be your fault!

FOUSTKA (*quietly to* VILMA): And then you'll be satisfied, won't you?

VILMA (*quietly*): Don't start that again.

FOUSTKA: I'm the one who started? Right?

DIRECTOR: Stop that! I'll ask at a higher level whether one of the local housing projects couldn't take her on as a cleaning lady.

LORENCOVA: I think that would be a very fortunate, humane, and sensible solution.

DIRECTOR (*to* FOUSTKA): Do you want to take advantage of your right to respond to the charges against you?

(FOUSTKA *stands up slowly and leans against the desk as if it were a speaker's podium.*)

FOUSTKA: Gentlemen, colleagues! I have complete faith in the objectivity and conscientiousness with which my case will be considered and I presume that at the right moment I will be given the opportunity to make an extensive explanation, and that certain circumstances with which I will acquaint you on that occasion will help prove my complete innocence. For the time being, therefore, I will confine myself to expressing the hope that the proceedings in this case—in keeping with our scientific approach to reality and our scientific morality—will be impartially and fully directed towards one goal alone: to discover the truth. This will further not only my own interests nor only the interests of science as such which this Institute is entrusted to guard and cultivate, but the interests of each of you as well. A different course of action, you see, might easily make my case merely the first link of a long chain of injustices the end of which I hardly dare contemplate. Thank you for your attention!

(FOUSTKA *sits down. An awkward pause. Everyone is slightly uneasy, albeit each for different reasons.*)

DIRECTOR: We're living in a modern day and age, and nobody here has any intention of staging any kind of witch-hunt. That would merely resurrect the same ancient ignorance and fanaticism against which we are battling, but in a new guise. Let the manner in which our colleague Foustka's case is resolved become an inspirational model of a truly scientific approach to the facts! The truth must prevail, come what may!

(*A short pause.*)

Who volunteered for garden clean-up?

KOTRLY: I did, Sir.

(*The* DIRECTOR *steps up to* KOTRLY. KOTRLY *stands up; the* DIRECTOR *places a hand on his shoulder and looks gravely into his eyes for a while.*)

DIRECTOR (*tenderly*): I'm glad you took the job, Vilem. I'll come to help you.

54

(MARKETA *enters through the left door, wearing a dress and carrying a small suitcase in her hand. Her face is tear-stained; she crosses the room as if sleepwalking and leaves through the rear door. Just as she closes it behind her, the chandelier crashes to the floor. It doesn't hit anyone but shatters into pieces on the floor.*)

The curtain falls.

Intermission

Scene 6

Foustka's apartment again. As the curtain rises, FISTULA *is alone on stage. He is sitting at the desk, going through the papers lying on it. He is wearing slippers, and the paper bag with his shoes in it is lying on the desk among the papers. After a while* FOUSTKA *enters, still in evening clothes. When he spots* FISTULA *he gives a start and cries out.*

FOUSTKA: What are you doing here?

FISTULA: I'm waiting for you.

FOUSTKA: How did you get in?

FISTULA: Not through the chimney, if that's what you're wondering. Through the door, which Mrs. Houbova kindly opened for me before she went out shopping, because I explained to her how urgently you needed to speak to me and how hard it would be for me to wait for you outside, what with my lame foot.

FOUSTKA: So you tricked her—how like you!

55

FISTULA: You don't believe that I'm a cripple?

FOUSTKA: My having to urgently speak to you is an out-and-out lie. Quite the contrary, after everything that happened I'd hoped I'd never see you again.

FISTULA: Quite the contrary, it's precisely *because* of what happened that our meeting has become many times more urgent.

FOUSTKA: And how dare you go through my papers!

FISTULA: Well, I had to do something to while away the time, didn't I?

FOUSTKA: And what about those shoes?

FISTULA: You make such a fuss about everything! (FISTULA *begins to grin stupidly, then he takes his bag, goes to the sofa, sits down, and places the bag beside him.*) Won't you sit down?

(FOUSTKA, *irritated, crosses to his desk, sits, and glares at* FISTULA.)

So what do you say to our success?

FOUSTKA: What success?

FISTULA: I never expected it to work so easily and so quickly. You're truly a gifted student.

FOUSTKA: I don't know what you're talking about!

FISTULA: You know perfectly well! We had agreed to do an innocent little experiment first, hadn't we? And that turned out to surpass our fondest expectations, don't you agree?

FOUSTKA: If you're referring to the fact that that unfortunate child developed a bit of a crush on me, then I'd like to say just two things. First, there was no magic involved, especially not yours; the only reason it happened was because it was the first time—

FISTULA: By pure chance—

FOUSTKA: That I actually had an opportunity to have a real talk with that young woman and because I happened to be—

FISTULA: By pure chance—

FOUSTKA: In pretty good form last night, so that my thoughts charmed her. Well, and as things seem to work with young girls, soon her interest was transferred—

FISTULA: By pure chance—

FOUSTKA: From what was being explained to the one who was explaining. I don't see anything about it that goes beyond the bounds of the ordinary. Second of all, seeing what happened to that poor child as a result of our conversation, my conscience is filled with heavy reproaches that it happened at all, even though I certainly never knew, and had no way of knowing, that our talk would have such consequences . . .

(FISTULA *begins to chortle and merrily slaps his thigh.*)

What's so funny about that?

FISTULA (*becomes serious*): My dear Doctor Foustka! Everybody knows that you don't believe in pure chance or coincidence. Don't you wonder how it happened that a person like you who could hardly stutter a request for a cup of coffee from that young woman until that moment suddenly found himself endowed with such impressive eloquence combined with the courage to express thoughts that are more than dangerous to express on the premises of your Institute? And doesn't it surprise you that it happened at just the very moment we had dreamed up our little idea? Honestly, aren't you a bit amazed at how your thoughts suddenly broke down that young woman's defenses—as if someone had waved a magic wand and allowed her to fall madly and indelibly in love in no time at all.

FOUSTKA: We all have moments in our lives when we seem to outdo ourselves.

FISTULA: That's just what I'm talking about!

FOUSTKA: I don't understand what you mean.

FISTULA: You didn't really expect Jeviel, the spirit of love, to arrive at your office party dressed in evening clothes all ready to fix everything up for you as if he were some sort of matchmaker? How else do you imagine he could do it than by means of your own self? He simply incorporated himself into you! Or rather, he simply awakened and liberated certain things that had always been dormant inside of you! Or to be even more precise, it was actually you yourself who decided to drop the reins restraining certain of your inner powers, and you yourself, therefore, who filled in for him, so to speak, or who fulfilled his intentions and thus won the day in his image, bearing his name!

FOUSTKA: There you are!

FISTULA: Of course a person isn't a static system of some sort—why you as a scientist must know that better than I. If a little seed is to sprout it must first be planted by someone.

FOUSTKA: If it's true that you and your . . .

FISTULA: Jeviel.

FOUSTKA: If you and your Jeviel are really responsible for planting this unfortunate seed, then I curse you from the

58

bottom of my heart! You're a devil and I don't want to have anything to do with you.

FISTULA: You're missing the point again! If the devil exists, then above all he exists within our own selves!

FOUSTKA: Then you, needless to say, must be his favorite residence!

FISTULA: You overestimate my value at least as much as you overestimated your own just a second ago. Think of it this way: I'm only a catalyst who helps his fellow creatures awaken or accelerate things that have long existed within themselves even without his help. My help, you see, merely enables them to discover their own courage to experience and enjoy something thrilling in life and consequently to become more fulfilled themselves! We only live once; why then should we spend those precious few decades that have been allotted to us stifling under the cover of some sort of philistine scruples? Do you know why you called me a devil? In order to shift your own responsibility—purely out of fear of your own scruples and of that thing within you that breaks them down—to a place outside of your own ego, in this case onto me, and by means of this "transference" as you scientists call it, or "projection," to ease your conscience! You hoped to fool your own scruples by using this kind of maneuver, and by assigning me that insulting name you hoped you'd actually even please them. But think of it this way, Doctor Foustka: I—a certain cripple, Fistula— wouldn't be able to move you an inch if you hadn't secretly dreamed about moving in that direction yourself long ago! Our little experiment had no other purpose than to clarify these little trivialities for you.

FOUSTKA: And what about your assurance that it was innocent? That was a dirty trick!

FISTULA: Wrong again! You're still only deceiving your own self! After all, you could have talked to the girl about the beauties of the scientific worldview and the worldwide significance of your Institute and she would have avoided any danger. But even after you did it the other way, you didn't have to abandon her so selfishly when things began to seem hopeless! But that's not the point now. There's one thing I've got to hand you, with my deepest compliments, especially since you're a beginner: your disguise—that classic tool of Jeviel's—in the pious habit of an ecstatic seeker after that one (*points his finger skyward*) as the true source of meaning of all creation and of all moral imperatives—that was truly brilliant! Congratulations!

FOUSTKA (*angrily*): What disguise? I was only saying what I believed!

FISTULA: My dear friend . . .

FOUSTKA: I'm not your friend!

FISTULA: My dear Sir, the truth isn't merely what we believe, after all, but also why and to whom and under what circumstances we say it!

(FOUSTKA *stares vacantly at* FISTULA *for a moment, then sadly nods his head, paces back and forth across the room a few times, and sits down again. After a while he begins to speak.*)

FOUSTKA (*quietly*): It's not altogether clear to me how they did it, but they sniffed out my contacts with you somehow, for which I'll most likely be fired from the Institute, punished as an example, publicly disgraced, and probably deprived of my livelihood and everything else. But certainly all this is merely superficial and immaterial, at least as far as I'm personally concerned. I see the true significance of what is in store for me as something else. It will be a deserved punishment for the unforgivable irresponsibility with which I behaved; for losing my moral vigilance and giving in to temptation, while under the poisonous influence of unjustified, malicious, and totally self-centered jealousy. I was trying to kill two birds with one stone and, in this way, hoping to win over one person and at the same time to wound another. I was truly blinded by something diabolical within me, and therefore I'm grateful to you for enabling me to have this experience, no matter how or why you did it. You simultaneously awakened both that temptation and that mean-spirited jealousy in me, and thus you made it possible for me to come to understand my own self better, especially my darkest sides. But that's not all. Your explanation has helped illuminate the true source of my doubt, which really does lie nowhere else but in my own self. Therefore I have no regrets about our meeting, if one can use that word to describe the way you forced yourself on me. It was an important lesson, and your dark designs have helped me discover a new inner light. I'm telling you this because it's my hope that we'll never see each other again, since I'm hoping that you'll leave this place immediately.

(A long pause. FISTULA slowly takes his shoes out of the bag, looks at them thoughtfully for a while, sniffs them, then finally places them on the ground in front of him and turns with a smile to FOUSTKA.)

FISTULA: Each of us is master of his own fate! I really wanted to mention something else, but now I'm not sure whether it wouldn't be better to wait for a time when you'll be in more of a—please pardon the expression—hot spot and, therefore, more receptive.

FOUSTKA: What did you want to mention?

FISTULA: I know that mechanism of thought rotation which

61

you just demonstrated as well as I know these shoes of mine! We sorcerers call it the Smichovsky Compensation Syndrome.

FOUSTKA: What's that?

FISTULA: When a novice first manages to break through the armor of his old defenses and opens himself up to the immense horizons of his hidden potential, after a little while something like a hangover sets in and he sinks into an almost masochistic state of self-accusation and self-punishment. Psychologically this emotional reaction is quite understandable: in an effort to mollify his betrayed scruples, almost as an afterthought, the novice mentally transforms the action through which he betrayed them into some sort of purifying lesson which he had to learn in order to become better. He makes of it, in short, a sort of small dance floor on which to perform ritual celebrations of his principles. It usually doesn't last long, and when he comes to his senses he recognizes what we, of course, knew from the start, but what we couldn't really explain to him: that is, the grotesque discrepancy between the dubious values in whose name he called down the most frightful punishment on himself, and the fundamental, existential significance of the experience that he is trying to atone for by means of this punishment.

(FOUSTKA *jumps up and angrily smashes the table.*)

FOUSTKA: That's it—now I've really had enough! If you think that all your high-flown oratory can get me tangled up in some new pseudoadventure, you're very much mistaken!

FISTULA: It's you who are very much mistaken if you think you aren't already tangled up . . .

FOUSTKA (*crying out*): Get out!

FISTULA: I'd just like to warn you that when you get back in touch with reality and suddenly feel the need for a consultation, I won't necessarily be available. But that's your business, after all . . .

FOUSTKA: Please—go away! I want to be alone with my Smichovsky Compensation Syndrome!

(FISTULA *slowly takes his shoes in his hands, all the while shaking his head in disbelief. Then, suddenly, he slams the shoes down on the floor, jumps up, and begins to wildly smack himself on the forehead.*)

FISTULA: I can hardly believe it! Because he dared to philosophize for a few minutes with another woman, his mistress throws a fit and denounces him for associating with a sorcerer.

FOUSTKA: What? That's a dirty lie!

FISTULA: And for that he'd be willing to give up his earnings, his scientific future, and maybe everything he owns without a fight! I've seen a lot of things, but this is a first! Smichovsky himself would have had his mind blown by this one!

FOUSTKA: I don't believe she'd stoop that low! After all those golden hours of sheer happiness we've had together!

FISTULA: Ah, what do you know about a woman's heart? Maybe the very memory of those hours provides the key to what she did! (FISTULA *calms down, sits down, slowly takes off his slippers, sniffs them, then carefully puts them away in his bag and begins to put on his shoes. A long pause.*)

FOUSTKA (*quietly*): And what, in your opinion, could I still do?

FISTULA: Let's not get into that.

FOUSTKA: Come on, tell me.

FISTULA: As you've probably realized, I don't give concrete advice and I don't make arrangements for anybody. At most I occasionally inspire . . . (*His shoes on, he grabs his bag with the slippers and heads for the door.*)

FOUSTKA (*screaming out*): Say it straight out, damn it!

(FISTULA *stops, stands completely still for a moment, and then turns to* FOUSTKA.)

FISTULA: It would be enough if you mobilized, in the name of a good cause, at least one thousandth of the cunning that your director mobilizes from morning till night in the name of a bad one!

(FISTULA *begins to grin stupidly.* FOUSTKA *stares at him with amazement.*)

The curtain falls.

Scene 7

The same room of the Institute in which Scenes 1 and 5 take place. Instead of the chandelier, a light bulb is suspended from an electrical wire. As the curtain rises, LORENCOVA, KOTRLY, *and* NEUWIRTH *are onstage.* LORENCOVA, *wearing a white coat, is sitting at the desk, a compact propped up against the typewriter, powdering her nose.* KOTRLY, *wearing a white coat, is sprawled out on the bench, reading the newspaper.* NEUWIRTH, *in civilian clothes, is standing at the rear by the bookcase, his back to the audience, examining a book. A short pause.*

LORENCOVA: What are we going to do about the coffee?

KOTRLY (*without looking up*): Why don't you make it?

LORENCOVA: Why don't you?

(FOUSTKA, *wearing a black sweater and black pants, quickly enters through the rear door, a briefcase in his hand, slightly out of breath.*)

FOUSTKA: Hi.

NEUWIRTH (*without turning around*): Hi.

(*No one reacts to Foustka's entrance; all continue doing what they were doing before. FOUSTKA sets his briefcase down on the desk and begins to take out various papers.*)

FOUSTKA: Were they here yet?

NEUWIRTH (*without turning around*): Not yet.

(*When FOUSTKA sees that LORENCOVA is not going to free the desk for him he crosses over to the bench where KOTRLY is sitting and sits down next to him. A pause.*)

LORENCOVA: Poor Marketa.

(FOUSTKA *looks up.*)

KOTRLY (*without looking up*): What's with her?

LORENCOVA: She tried to slit her wrists.

(FOUSTKA *stands up, shaken.*)

KOTRLY (*without turning around*): So it's true after all?

NEUWIRTH (*without turning around*): They say she's in the psychiatric ward.

LORENCOVA: Poor thing.

(FOUSTKA *sits down again. The* DEPUTY, *in everyday clothes, and* PETRUSHKA, *in a white coat, enter through the right door,*

65

holding hands. LORENCOVA *shoves the compact into her coat pocket.* KOTRLY *folds his newspaper.* NEUWIRTH *puts aside the book and turns around.* LORENCOVA, KOTRLY, *and* FOUSTKA *stand up.*)

KOTRLY: Good morning, Sir.

DEPUTY: Hello there, my friends! And please sit down.

(LORENCOVA, KOTRLY, *and* FOUSTKA *sit down again. A short pause.*)

I don't see Vilma here.

FOUSTKA: She's at the dentist.

(*Short pause.*)

DEPUTY: As you well know, the task we're facing today is not an easy one. Nobody here—as our director said so nicely—has any intention of staging a witch-hunt. The truth must prevail, come what may. But for that very reason we must remind ourselves that looking for the truth means looking for the whole, unadulterated truth. That is to say that the truth isn't only something that can be demonstrated in one way or another, it is also the purpose for which the demonstrated thing is used or for which it may be misused, and who boasts about it and why, and in what context it finds itself. As scientists we know well that by tearing a certain fact out of its context we can not only completely shift or change its meaning, but we can stand it right on its head and thus make a lie out of the truth or vice versa. In short, then, we shouldn't allow the living background of the acts with which we are going to concern ourselves to disappear from our field of vision, nor the conclusions which we will draw about them. I hope I don't have to elaborate any further—we aren't little children, damn it! Or are we?

66

KOTRLY: We aren't.

DEPUTY: So there you are! Who's feeding the carrier pigeons today?

NEUWIRTH: I am.

DEPUTY: Splendid!

(*The* DIRECTOR, *wearing a white coat, enters through the right door.* LORENCOVA, KOTRLY, *and* FOUSTKA *rise immediately.*)

KOTRLY: Hi.

DIRECTOR: Hello there, my friends! And please sit down.

(LORENCOVA, KOTRLY, *and* FOUSTKA *sit down. A short pause.*)

I don't see Vilma.

DEPUTY: I didn't see her either when I came. She's apparently at the dentist.

(*The* DIRECTOR *approaches* KOTRLY *and holds out his hand.* KOTRLY *rises.*)

DIRECTOR (*to* KOTRLY): Did you get a good night's sleep?

KOTRLY: Very good, thank you.

(*The* DIRECTOR *presses Kotrly's elbow in a friendly manner and turns to the others.* KOTRLY *sits down.*)

DIRECTOR: As you well know, the task we're facing today is not an easy one.

DEPUTY: That's precisely what I was telling our colleagues just a second ago, Sir!

DIRECTOR: We all know the issue, so we can skip the preliminaries . . .

(VILMA, *out of breath, and carrying a large paper box in her hand, rushes in through the rear door.*)

VILMA: Please excuse me, Sir, I'm very sorry . . . I had an appointment at the dentist this morning, and can you imagine, I—

DIRECTOR: I know about it, sit down.

(VILMA *sits on the oilcloth couch, places the box at her feet, communicates something through gestures to* FOUSTKA, *and then shows that she is crossing her fingers for him.* LORENCOVA *leans over to her.*)

LORENCOVA (*quietly*): What's this?

VILMA (*quietly*): A toaster from the repair shop.

LORENCOVA (*quietly*): I thought it was a new hat.

VILMA (*quietly*): No.

DIRECTOR: Where was I?

KOTRLY: You were saying that we can skip the preliminaries . . .

DIRECTOR: Ah yes. So we can skip the preliminaries and get right to the subject. Doctor Foustka, if you would kindly . . .

(*The* DIRECTOR *motions to* FOUSTKA *to come to the front.* FOUSTKA *rises, crosses to the middle of the room, and stands in the place where the* DIRECTOR *has indicated.*)

There, that's good. Shall we begin?

FOUSTKA: Certainly.

DIRECTOR: Well, then, could you tell us, my friend, whether it's true that for some time now . . .

(At that moment the SECRET MESSENGER enters through the right door, steps up to the DIRECTOR, and whispers something at length in his ear. The DIRECTOR gravely nods his head. After a longer while the SECRET MESSENGER concludes. The DIRECTOR nods his head one last time. The SECRET MESSENGER exits through the right door.)

Where was I?

KOTRLY: You were asking him whether it's true that for some time now . . .

DIRECTOR: Ah yes. Well, then, could you tell us, Sir, whether it's true that for some time now you've been engaged in the study of what's known as occult literature?

FOUSTKA: It's true.

DIRECTOR: For how long?

FOUSTKA: I don't know exactly . . .

DIRECTOR: A round number will do. A half a year? A year?

FOUSTKA: Something like that.

DIRECTOR: How many such books, in your estimation, did you read in that period?

FOUSTKA: I didn't count them.

DIRECTOR: A round number will do. Five? Thirty? Fifty?

FOUSTKA: Maybe fifty.

DIRECTOR: To whom did you lend them out?

FOUSTKA: No one.

DIRECTOR: Now, now, Sir, you aren't going to tell us that nobody borrowed such desirable and rare books from you,

69

books impossible to come by these days! Your friends obviously had to see them at your place.

FOUSTKA: I don't invite friends over to my place, and I never lend books.

DIRECTOR: Very well, then. And now please concentrate— this is an important question: what led you to these studies? Why, actually, did you begin a systematic investigation of these things?

FOUSTKA: I'd been uneasy for a long time about our young people's mounting interest in everything that has anything to do with the so-called supernatural. As a result of this uneasiness of mine I gradually decided to write a brochure in which I would try to demonstrate, by means of mysticism itself, how incongruous that conglomeration of twisted fragments from various cultural circles is, and how strikingly inconsistent these various idealistic and mystical theories of the past are with contemporary scientific knowledge. At the same time I especially chose mysticism as the subject for my critical attention rather than any other because of the uncritical interest it is enjoying today. My project, of course, required—

DIRECTOR (*interrupting*): None of us doubted, Sir, that you would answer that question precisely as you did. But in the meanwhile, none of us knows how you intend to explain the shocking fact that you allegedly practiced black magic yourself.

FOUSTKA: I didn't really practice it much; mostly I just spread the word that I did.

DIRECTOR: Why?

FOUSTKA: Because that was the only way to build trust among people as mistrustful as today's sorcerers are.

DIRECTOR: So you craved their trust? Interesting, interesting! How far did you get in achieving it?

FOUSTKA: So far I've been only modestly successful, my success taking the form of a certain source who visited me two times, about whom you have been informed.

DIRECTOR: Did that source tell you why it sought you out?

FOUSTKA: Apparently it knew about my interest in the practice of black magic and was willing to initiate me into it.

DIRECTOR: Did you agree to that?

FOUSTKA: Not expressly, but at the same time I didn't expressly refuse. We're in a state of so-called mutual discussion.

DIRECTOR: What does it want in return?

FOUSTKA: For me to testify that it put itself at the disposal of science, if the need arises.

DEPUTY: Do you hear that, Sir! What a cunning bunch they are!

DIRECTOR: It seems to me, Foustka, that it's high time to ask our pivotal question: how do you explain the fact that on the one hand you claim to have a scientific viewpoint, and consequently must know that black magic is sheer charlatanism, while on the other hand you're trying to gain the trust of sorcerers, and when one of them actually seeks you out, not only do you *not* kick him out and laugh in his face, but on the contrary, you make plans to collaborate with him, and indeed, even to cover up for him? You'll surely find it hard to explain these murky contacts and activities by invoking scientific-critical interests.

71

FOUSTKA: It may seem foolish to you, but I simply felt from the very first that my efforts to help those seduced by charlatans and my intentions to fight effectively against such seducers must not be confined to mere theoretical-propagandistic work. I was and am to this day convinced that it wouldn't be honest to keep my hands entirely clear of living reality in an effort to keep them clean, as it were, and to lull my conscience with illusions about God knows what great practical results coming out of my theoretical struggle. I simply felt that if you start something you're obliged to finish it, and that it is my civic duty to put my theoretical knowledge in the service of the practical struggle, which means concretely searching for the hotbed of those activities, and then uncovering and convicting the perpetrators. Why, we're constantly boasting about our battle against fakery, mysticism, and superstition, but if we had to point a finger at even a single disseminator of these poisons, we couldn't do it! But not just us—it's almost unbelievable how little success anybody has had in infiltrating those areas, and thanks to that, how little is known about them! Small wonder, then, that they're spreading so rampantly. That's why I decided to win the confidence of those circles, infiltrate them, and there, in the field, to gather evidence of their guilt! Which of course I couldn't do without pretending to have at least partial belief in their spirits, initiations, evocations, magical spells, incubi, and succubi and all that other rubbish. I'd probably even be forced to swear oaths of silence or provide eventual cover-ups. In short, I decided to enlist as an inconspicuous and possibly solitary soldier in this silent war, as one might call it, because I arrived at the conclusion that my expertise put me under a direct obligation to do so. We're dealing, you see, with a sphere in which, unfortunately, a so-called broad perspective is still considered valuable, if not an actual prerequisite for any participation in its life.

(*A long pause. Everyone present is stunned, each looks in confusion at the others, then finally all looks come to center on the* DIRECTOR.)

DIRECTOR: So that you actually . . . I see . . . I see . . . (*Pause.*) Well, in fact, it wouldn't be such a bad thing if our Institute could pull off a truly concrete victory like that! Our colleague Foustka is right about one thing, brochures have never won wars.

DEPUTY (*to* FOUSTKA): You would therefore be willing, if I understand you correctly, to provide us with notes about each of your encounters, whether with that source of yours or with any others.

FOUSTKA: Of course! That's exactly why I'm doing it!

DEPUTY: That wouldn't be such a bad thing, as our director has already pointed out. But just one thing isn't clear to me: why did we have to hear about your praiseworthy initiative only now, after certain unfair—as it turns out—accusations have been leveled against you? Why didn't you yourself keep us informed right from the start about your decision and your first steps?

FOUSTKA: I see now that it was a mistake. But I looked at it in a completely different way. As a researcher who is inexperienced in hands-on fieldwork, I unconsciously compared my role to the situation of an independent scientific worker, who doesn't keep a running account of each of his professional moves either. I thought that it would be sufficient—just as it is in theoretical work—to write a report about my work only at the point where there is really something to report about, that is, when I actually had something concretely relevant and useful in hand. It absolutely never crossed my mind that some chance information about my

73

activities from someone uninformed about their purpose might in some way shake the confidence that I had hitherto enjoyed here.

DIRECTOR: You really can't be surprised at that, Foustka. Your decision, however noble-minded, is unfortunately so unusual, and, truth to tell, so totally unexpected from you of all people, that logically our first conclusions were more likely to be on the negative side.

DEPUTY: You really can't be surprised at that, Dr. Foustka.

DIRECTOR: Never mind—let's come to some sort of conclusion, then. You've convinced me that this was all a sheer misunderstanding, and I'm glad that everything was cleared up so quickly. Needless to say, I think highly of your brave decision and I can assure you that this work of yours will be prized all the more for it, especially once you get in the habit of keeping thorough records of it and simultaneously keeping us informed. Does anyone have anything further to add? (*An awkward pause.*) Nobody does? In that case, the time has come for a small surprise: tomorrow's get-together at the Institute garden will be a costume party!

LORENCOVA: Bravo!

KOTRLY: A great idea!

DEPUTY: Oh, yes! I like it a lot too.

LORENCOVA: And what theme will it have?

DIRECTOR: Isn't it obvious? A witches' sabbath!

(*A wave of commotion runs through the room.*)

A gathering of devils, witches, sorcerers, and magicians. Classy, what? Originally I only saw it as an attempt to liven up the office party tradition with a certain parodistic element. It seemed to me that if at night we made fun of the very thing we have to fight against so seriously and soberly during the day, we could—in the spirit of modern group-costume therapy—enhance our relationship to our own work. Simply by treating the problem with frivolity for a few moments we would emphasize its permanent unfrivolity, by making light of it we would emphasize its gravity, by stepping away from it we would get closer to it. Now, however, thanks to a timely coincidence, I think we can see it in yet another way: as a playful tribute to the work of our colleague Foustka here, who not only needs to find a disguise, in the metaphorical sense of the word, but also may face the unenviable task of finding a literal disguise soon—on that occasion when he decides to infiltrate some actual black mass or other! (*Polite laughter.*) Ah well, let's all look at it— at least in part—as a sort of jolly little ending to the serious transaction we just concluded! Who's feeding the carrier pigeons today?

NEUWIRTH: I am.

DIRECTOR: Splendid! (*To* KOTRLY:) Vilem, don't forget!

The curtain falls.

Scene 8

Vilma's apartment again. As the curtain rises, FOUSTKA, *wearing undershorts, is sitting on the bed, and* VILMA, *wearing a slip, is combing her hair at the mirror—the situation is the same as at the beginning of Scene 4.*

FOUSTKA: I just bet you could buy him off with a mere kiss on

75

the cheek, once he was in the house! Surely he tried to dance with you at the very least!

VILMA: Henry, drop it, for goodness sake! I don't keep pumping you for details either—and I'd have far more reason to do so!

(*A short pause. Then* FOUSTKA *gets up and begins to walk back and forth, deep in thought.* VILMA *stops combing her hair and looks at him in surprise.*)

What's wrong?

FOUSTKA: What should be wrong?

VILMA: You began so well.

FOUSTKA: Somehow I'm not in the mood for it today.

VILMA: Does it arouse you too much?

FOUSTKA: It's not that.

VILMA: So what happened?

FOUSTKA: You know very well.

VILMA: I don't!

FOUSTKA: You really don't know? And who denounced me to the director about the sorcerer coming to see me, you don't know that either?

(VILMA *freezes, then throws down the comb, jumps up excitedly, and looks at* FOUSTKA *with astonishment.*)

VILMA: For God's sake, Henry, you don't think that—

FOUSTKA: Nobody else at the Institute knew about it!

VILMA: Are you crazy? Why would I do it, for goodness sake? If you're going to insult me with the thought that I could

76

denounce anybody at all to that imbecile, how can you imagine that I'd go and denounce *you?* Why, that would be as bad as denouncing my own self! You know how much I want you to be happy, and how I'm constantly worrying about you! How could I possibly want to destroy you all of a sudden? And my own self at the same time—our relationship—our life together—our make-believe jealousy games—our love—so marvelously confirmed by those flashes of true jealousy that you've begun to show in recent days, our memories of all those golden hours of sheer happiness we've had together—why, it would be pure madness!

FOUSTKA: What if it were precisely the memory of those golden hours that provided the key to such an act? What do I know about a woman's heart? Maybe you wanted to get even with me over Marketa—or maybe it was just fear of that cripple and an effort to save me from what you thought were his clutches in this way.

(VILMA *runs to the bed, throws herself face down on the pillows, and begins to sob desperately.* FOUSTKA *doesn't know what to do. He looks at* VILMA *helplessly for a while, then sits down beside her cautiously and begins to stroke her hair.*)

Come on, Vilma.

(*Pause.* VILMA *sobs.*)

I didn't mean it that way.

(*Pause.* VILMA *sobs.*)

I was just kidding.

(*Pause.* VILMA *sobs.*)

I just wanted to try a new game.

(*Pause.* VILMA *suddenly sits up briskly, dries her eyes with a handkerchief, and snuffles her nose to clear it. When she feels herself sufficiently calm and strong she speaks coldly.*)

VILMA: Go away!

(FOUSTKA *tries to stroke her; she pushes him away and cries out.*)

Don't touch me—just go!

FOUSTKA: Vilma! I didn't say anything all that terrible! How many times did you want me to tell you far more terrible things!

VILMA: That was different. Are you even aware of what you just did? Why, you actually accused me of being a stool pigeon. I'm asking you to get dressed, to leave, and never to try to repair what you just destroyed so brutally!

FOUSTKA: Are you serious?

VILMA: At least we'll have it over with. It would have happened sooner or later in any case!

FOUSTKA: Because of that dancer?

VILMA: No.

FOUSTKA: Why, then?

VILMA: I'm beginning to lose my respect for you.

FOUSTKA: This is the first I've heard of it.

VILMA: It doesn't take long to happen, you know. I actually realized it only today, when I saw the way you saved your neck at the Institute. Offering the director to inform for him, and so shamelessly, in front of everybody! And now, to top it all off, you, a voluntary and self-declared stool pigeon, dare to accuse me, innocent and devoted me, of inform-

78

ing—and what's more, of informing on you! Do you see how absurd it is? What's happened to you? What's gotten into you? Are you actually the same person anymore? Maybe you really *are* possessed by some devil! That fellow addled your brains. God knows what stuff he told you. God knows what spell he cast on you.

(FOUSTKA *gets up and begins to walk back and forth across the room in agitation.*)

FOUSTKA: For your information he doesn't cast spells, he only helps people understand their own selves better and face all the bad things dormant inside them! Furthermore, about my being a stool pigeon, as you put it, not only was that the only way I could save myself, it was also the only way I could help him as well! If they believe that I'm controlling him, they'll leave him alone. And the third thing, my suspecting that they found out about him from you—I simply couldn't hide it from you. What would that have done to our relationship! You might have said something unintentionally—in front of someone you trusted by mistake—or somebody could have accidentally overheard you . . .

VILMA: I never said anything intentionally or not, and what bothers me about your suspicions is not your speaking up about them, or even that you spoke up so crudely, which you're now belatedly trying to make up for, but that they occurred to you at all! If you're capable of thinking something like that about me for even a split second, then there's really no point in our staying together.

(*Pause.* FOUSTKA *sits down dejectedly in the armchair and stares dully into space.*)

FOUSTKA: I was a fool to say anything to you. I always spoil everything so stupidly. What am I going to do without you? I can't stand myself.

VILMA: And now you're even feeling sorry for yourself!

FOUSTKA: Do you remember what we said to each other that time under the elms at the riverbank?

VILMA: Don't drag those elms into this, it won't do you any good. You've hurt me too much to talk your way out of it by manipulating our memories of the past. And besides, I asked you to do something . . .

FOUSTKA: You mean that I should leave?

VILMA: Exactly!

FOUSTKA: You're expecting the dancer, aren't you?

VILMA: I'm not expecting anyone, I simply want to be alone!

(*A short pause. Then* FOUSTKA *suddenly jumps up, runs over to* VILMA, *knocks her down roughly on the bed, and grabs her wildly by the neck.*)

FOUSTKA (*in a dark voice*): You're lying, you whore!

VILMA (*crying out in terror*): Help!

(FOUSTKA *begins to strangle* VILMA. *Just then the doorbell rings.* FOUSTKA *drops* VILMA *immediately, jumps away from her in confusion, stands there for a moment helplessly, then slowly heads for the armchair and lowers himself into it heavily.* VILMA *stands up, quickly straightens herself up a bit, goes to the door, and opens it. There stands the* DANCER, *holding a bunch of violets behind his back.*)

DANCER: Excuse me for disturbing you so late, I only wanted to bring you these. (*The* DANCER *hands* VILMA *the violets.*)

VILMA: Thanks! Come in, please, and stay a while . . .

(*The* DANCER *looks at* VILMA *in surprise, and then at* FOUSTKA

80

collapsed in the armchair staring absently into space. An awkward pause.)

He's not feeling well, you see—I'm a little worried.

DANCER: Some sort of heart trouble?

VILMA: Probably.

DANCER: So in the meanwhile we could dance a little bit, what do you say? Maybe it would distract him.

The curtain falls.

Scene 9

Foustka's apartment again. As the curtain rises, FOUSTKA is alone onstage. Dressed in a dressing gown, he is pacing back and forth, deep in thought. After a long while someone knocks at the door. FOUSTKA stops in his tracks, hesitates for a moment, and then calls.

FOUSTKA: Who is it?

HOUBOVA (*offstage*): It's me, Doctor Foustka.

FOUSTKA (*calling*): Come in, Mrs. Houbova.

HOUBOVA (*entering*): You've got a visitor.

FOUSTKA: I do? Who?

HOUBOVA: Well, it's him again . . . you know . . . the one that . . .

FOUSTKA: That smells?

HOUBOVA: Yes.

FOUSTKA: Show him in.

(*A short pause;* HOUBOVA *stands uncertainly.*)

What's the matter?

HOUBOVA: Doctor Foustka . . .

FOUSTKA: Did something happen?

HOUBOVA: I'm just a stupid woman. I know it's not my place to give you advice about anything.

FOUSTKA: What's on your mind?

HOUBOVA: I'm sorry, but if I were in your place I wouldn't trust that fellow! I can't really explain it—I don't even know what business he has with you—I just have a sort of strange feeling about him.

FOUSTKA: Last time you let him in yourself!

HOUBOVA: Because I was scared of him.

FOUSTKA: I'll admit he looks disreputable, but basically he's harmless. Or, to be more precise, he's too insignificant to do any serious damage.

HOUBOVA: Do you have to associate with people like him? You?

FOUSTKA: Mrs. Houbova, I'm a grown-up and I know what I'm doing, after all!

HOUBOVA: But I'm so worried about you! Don't you see, I remember you as a three-year-old. I don't have children of my own . . .

FOUSTKA: Of course, that's fine, I'm really grateful for your concern. I understand and I appreciate it, but I think that in this case it's really unnecessary. Show him in and don't worry about it anymore.

(HOUBOVA *exits, leaving the door ajar.*)

HOUBOVA (*offstage*): This way, Mister.

(FISTULA *enters, carrying his bag in his hand.* HOUBOVA *takes one last look after him into the room, shakes her head anxiously, and closes the door.* FISTULA, *grinning stupidly, rushes directly to the sofa, sits down, takes off his shoes, takes his slippers out of the bag and puts them on, puts the shoes into the bag, which he then places on the sofa beside him. He looks up at* FOUSTKA *and begins to grin.*)

FISTULA: So, what?

FOUSTKA: What, what?

FISTULA: I'm waiting for you to begin your usual song and dance.

FOUSTKA: What song and dance?

FISTULA: That I should leave immediately and so on.

(FOUSTKA *walks around the room, deep in thought, then sits at his desk.*)

FOUSTKA: Listen! In the first place, I've come to understand that it's impossible simply to get rid of you and therefore it makes no sense to waste time trying to do something that's doomed to failure in advance. In the second place, without making too much of your inspirational influence, as you call it, I've come to the conclusion that time spent with you doesn't have to be a complete waste after all. If I have to be a subject for you, why, then, shouldn't you be a subject for me in turn? Or isn't that how your original proposal went: that you offer me an inside look at your practices, for which I, in exchange, guarantee you a certain cover? I've decided to accept your proposal.

FISTULA: I knew you'd work yourself up to it, which was one of the reasons for my persistence. I'm glad that my persistence is finally rewarded. But not to be too humble about it, again: I don't attribute your decision to my persistence alone, but also to the obvious accomplishments our collaboration has achieved . . .

FOUSTKA: What accomplishments are you referring to now?

FISTULA: Not only that you kept your job at the Institute, but that you actually even improved your position there. Meanwhile, it gives me great joy to state that in this particular case you even managed to avoid Smichovsky's Compensatory Syndrome, which is a sign of real progress.

FOUSTKA: If you're trying to suggest that I lost all my moral values and gave in to whatever it is that you're trying to awaken inside of me, then you are very much mistaken. I'm still the same person. I'm just cooler and more in control as a result of my recent experiences, which allows me to know at all times just how far and in which direction—however new it might be for me—I am able to go, without the risk of letting myself in for something that I might bitterly regret later on.

(FISTULA *grows slightly uneasy, fidgets a bit, looks around.*)

What's the matter with you?

FISTULA: Oh nothing, nothing.

FOUSTKA: You look like you're afraid, which is a condition I don't recognize in you and which would especially surprise me after the explicit promise of cover I just gave you.

(FISTULA *takes off his slippers and rubs the soles of his feet with both hands, sighing all the while.*)

Does it hurt?

FISTULA: It's nothing, it'll go away. (*After a while he puts on his slippers again. Then he suddenly begins to cackle.*)

FOUSTKA: What's so funny now?

FISTULA: May I be completely frank?

FOUSTKA: Suit yourself.

FISTULA: You are!

FOUSTKA: What? You find me funny? What nerve!

(FISTULA *grows serious and stares at the ground. After a while he suddenly glances up at* FOUSTKA.)

FISTULA: Look here, Doctor Foustka. The fact that you saved your neck by means of a little dirty work is quite all right. Why, Hajaha and I—

FOUSTKA: Who?

FISTULA: Hajaha, the spirit of politics—we were pointing you in that very direction! What's not quite all right is that in the process you forgot the rules of the game!

FOUSTKA: What rules? What game? What the devil are you talking about?

FISTULA: Don't you suppose that our work together has rules of its own too? Break down your own scruples as much as you want—as you know, I always welcome that sort of thing on principle. But to double-cross the very one who is leading you along this thrilling and, I might even say, revolutionary path—that, you really shouldn't do! Even a revolution has its laws! Last time you called me a devil. Imagine for a moment that I really were one! How do you suppose I'd react to your amateurish attempt to deceive me?

FOUSTKA: But I'm not trying to deceive you.

FISTULA: Look, without actually making any explicit promises, we certainly reached a sort of unspoken agreement not to talk about our work together with anyone, much less make reports on it to hostile and threatening authorities. One might even go so far as to say that we had begun—naturally with some caution—to trust each other. If you failed to understand the inner meaning of our agreement and you decided to thumb your nose at it, that was your first serious mistake. You've done enough reading, after all, to know that there are certain limits—even in my sphere—that you can't overstep; in fact, precisely here, with so much at stake, the commandment against overstepping them is especially severe. Don't you understand that if we're capable of playing around with the whole world, it is only and entirely because we depend on contacts that we're absolutely forbidden to play around with? To deceive a liar is fine, to deceive a truth teller is still allowable, but to deceive the very instrument that gives us the strength to deceive and that allows us in advance to deceive with impunity—that, you truly cannot expect to get away with! That one (*points skyward*), overwhelms Man with a multitude of unkeepable commandments, and therefore there's nothing left for him but to forgive occasionally. The others, on the other hand, liberate Man from all those unkeepable commandments, and therefore, understandably, they are totally rid of the need, opportunity, and, finally, even the capacity to forgive. But even if that weren't so, they wouldn't be able to forgive the betrayal of the very agreement releasing all that boundless freedom. Why, such forgiveness would make their entire world collapse! But really, might not the obligation to be faithful to the authority which gives us that sort of freedom actually be the only guarantee of freedom from all obligation? Do you see what I mean?

(FOUSTKA, *who has been growing increasingly nervous during Fistula's speech, stands up and begins to pace about the room. A long pause.* FISTULA *watches him carefully. Then* FOUSTKA *suddenly comes to a stop at his desk, leans against it as if against a speaker's podium, and turns to* FISTULA.)

FOUSTKA: I see what you mean perfectly well, but I'm afraid you don't see what *I* mean!

FISTULA: Is that so?

FOUSTKA: You can look at the promise you're obviously referring to as an attempt to betray you only because you don't know why I made it and was able to make it with a clear conscience!

FISTULA: You made it in order to save your neck.

FOUSTKA: Of course, but what good would it be if the price were betrayal! I'm not that stupid! The only reason that I was able to make the promise was because I was determined right from the start not only *not* to keep it, but at the same time to cleverly use the position it gained for me—naturally in close consultation with you—for our purposes and to our advantage. In other words, to gain control over their information, while flooding them with our own disinformation; to erase the real tracks, while keeping them busy with false ones; to use their own organization to rescue those of us who are threatened, while drowning those who threaten us. And with all this, to serve our cause by being our own man hidden in the heart of the enemy, indeed, in the very heart of the enemy's division specifically designed to fight against us! I'm surprised and disappointed that you didn't understand and appreciate my plan immediately.

(FOUSTKA *sits.* FISTULA *leaps up and begins to cackle and jump around the room wildly. Then he suddenly stops and quite matter-of-factly turns to* FOUSTKA.)

FISTULA: Even if you just invented this conceit, I'll still accept it, if only to give you one last chance. Actually it *is* possible to forgive, and to give people a chance to make amends, even in our realm. If I claimed the opposite a little while ago, it was only to scare you into coming out with precisely the sort of unambiguous offer as the one you just made, thereby allowing you to save yourself at the very edge of the abyss. But obviously, and luckily for you, I'm really not the devil. He would never have let you get away with the betrayal that I just let you get away with, never!

(FOUSTKA *is visibly relieved, can't hide it, goes to* FISTULA *and embraces him.* FISTULA *jumps aside, his teeth begin to chatter, and he begins to quickly rub his arms.*)

Man, you must be a hundred below zero!

FOUSTKA (*laughing*): Not quite.

The curtain falls.

Scene 10

The Institute garden once again. Except that the bench is now on the right and the table with drinks now on the left, everything is exactly the same as it was in Scene 3, including the lighting. As the curtain rises, the music becomes quiet and changes in style just as at the beginning of Scene 3. This time, too, it will provide a background for the entire scene unless otherwise indicated. The two LOVERS and FOUSTKA are onstage. The LOVERS dance together in the background, where they will continue to dance without interruption for almost the entire scene, leaving their bower empty for now. FOUSTKA is sitting on the bench, deep in thought. All three are wearing costumes that suit the "magic" theme of the party. FOUSTKA *is wearing the traditional theatrical costume for Faust. All characters appearing in this scene are dressed or in some cases painted in this same spirit. Some of the best-known and most common motifs traditionally used in the theater for "hellish" or "witchlike" themes should make an appearance in this scene; for instance, the colors red and black should predominate, as well as a profusion of pendants and amulets of various sorts, wildly tangled women's wigs, devils' tails, hoofs, and chains, etc. A long pause. Then, from the right,* LORENCOVA *emerges with a broom under her arm. She crosses the stage towards the table, where she pours herself a drink. Pause.*

FOUSTKA: Do you happen to know if the director is here yet?

LORENCOVA: No I don't.

(*Pause.* LORENCOVA *finishes her drink, puts the glass down, and vanishes to the left. After a while she can be seen in the background, dancing alone with her broom. Pause. Then the* DEPUTY *enters from the left.*)

DEPUTY: Have you seen Petrushka?

FOUSTKA: She hasn't been here.

(*The* DEPUTY *shakes his head uncomprehendingly and vanishes to the right. After a while he may be seen in the background, swaying alone to the dance music.* FOUSTKA *gets up and goes to the table, where he pours himself a drink. The* DIRECTOR *and* KOTRLY, *holding hands, enter from the right. Unless otherwise noted, they will be holding hands for the whole scene. The* DIRECTOR, *in a particularly conspicuous devil costume, has horns on his head. The* DIRECTOR *and* KOTRLY *pay no attention to* FOUSTKA *and stop in the middle of the stage.* FOUSTKA, *at the table, watches them.*)

DIRECTOR (*to* KOTRLY): Where will you actually put it? Around here?

KOTRLY: I thought I'd put it in the bower.

DIRECTOR: All right. That would be better for safety reasons too.

KOTRLY: I'll light it in the gardener's shed, then I'll secretly bring it here—it takes a few minutes to warm up. I'll set it down in the bower, and a little while later you'll see . . . (DIRECTOR *and* KOTRLY *head towards the left.*)

FOUSTKA: Excuse me, Sir . . .

(*The* DIRECTOR *and* KOTRLY *stop.*)

DIRECTOR: Yes, Foustka?

FOUSTKA: I wonder if you have a minute or two?

DIRECTOR: I'm sorry, Foustka, but certainly not now.

(*The* DIRECTOR *and* KOTRLY *disappear to the left. After a while they may be seen in the background, dancing together.* FOUSTKA, *holding his glass, crosses back to the bench, deep in thought, and sits down. The music grows noticeably louder, some well-known tango may be heard, for instance, "Tango Milonga."* VILMA *and the* DANCER *rush onstage from the left and begin to do some complicated tango figures together. These are choreographed mainly by the* DANCER, *obviously a professional, who continues to glide about the stage elaborately and skillfully with* VILMA. FOUSTKA *stares at them in astonishment. After a while the tango comes to a climax and* VILMA *and the* DANCER *do a closing figure. The music grows softer and changes its character. Out of breath but happy,* VILMA *and the* DANCER *are holding hands and smiling at each other.*)

FOUSTKA: Are you enjoying yourselves?

VILMA: As you can see.

(*The* DEPUTY, *who has in the interim left the dance floor, enters from the left.*)

DEPUTY: Have you seen Petrushka?

VILMA: She hasn't been here.

(*The* DEPUTY *shakes his head impatiently and vanishes to the right. After a while he may be seen in the background, swaying alone to the dance music.* VILMA *seizes the* DANCER *by the hand and leads him away. They both disappear to the left. After a while they may be seen in the background, dancing.* FOUSTKA *stands up, crosses to the table, and pours himself a drink. The* DIRECTOR *and* KOTRLY, *who have in the interim disappeared from the dance floor, enter from the right, holding hands. They pay no attention to* FOUSTKA *but stop in the middle of the stage.* FOUSTKA, *at the table, watches them.*)

KOTRLY (*to the* DIRECTOR): How will I know when it's the right time for it?

DIRECTOR: You'll figure it out somehow, or else I'll give you a signal. I'm worried about something else.

KOTRLY: What?

DIRECTOR: Can you really guarantee that nothing will go wrong?

KOTRLY: What should go wrong?

DIRECTOR: Well, somebody might suffocate—or something might catch fire . . .

KOTRLY: Don't worry.

(*The* DIRECTOR *and* KOTRLY *head towards the left.*)

FOUSTKA: Excuse me, Sir . . .

DIRECTOR: Yes, Foustka?

FOUSTKA: I realize that you have a lot of other things on your mind just now, but I won't keep you long, and I'm certain that the thing I want to talk to you about will interest you.

DIRECTOR: I'm sorry, but now it's really impossible . . .

(*Just then the* SECRET MESSENGER *enters from the right, goes up to the* DIRECTOR, *leans over, and whispers in his ear at length. The* DIRECTOR *nods his head. While the* MESSENGER *is whispering,* LORENCOVA, *who has in the interim left the dance floor, enters from the right holding her broom in her hand. She remains standing near the bench and gazes at the* MESSENGER. *After a long while the* MESSENGER *concludes. The* DIRECTOR *nods one last time, at which point he disappears to the left with* KOTRLY. *After a while they may be seen in the background, dancing together. The* MESSENGER *heads towards the right, just opposite* LORENCOVA. *She is smiling at him. He stops directly in front of her. For a moment both of them stare at each other intently, then the* MESSENGER, *without taking his eyes off her, takes her broom from her hand, places it on the ground meaningfully, and commences to embrace* LORENCOVA. *She embraces him in return. For a moment they gaze meltingly into each other's eyes, then they begin to kiss. When they move apart after a while, they disappear together to the right, arms around each other's waists. After a while they may be seen in the background, dancing.* FOUSTKA, *glass in hand and deep in thought, crosses the stage to the bench and sits down. Suddenly, he becomes attentive and listens. Offstage a girl's voice may be heard, singing the melody of the music that is just playing, Ophelia's song from* Hamlet.)

MARKETA (*singing offstage*):
    And will 'a not come again?
    And will 'a not come again?
    No, no, he is dead,
    Go to thy death bed,

(MARKETA *emerges at left. She is barefoot, her hair is loose and flowing; on her head is a wreath made of wild flowers. She is wearing a white nightgown with the word "psychiatry" stamped at the bottom in large letters. She approaches* FOUSTKA *slowly, singing. He rises, aghast.*)

> He never will come again.
> His beard was as white as snow
> All flaxen was his poll
> He is gone, he is gone,
> And we cast away moan.
> God 'a' mercy on his soul!

FOUSTKA (*crying out*): Marketa!

MARKETA: Oh where is that handsome Prince of Denmark?

(FOUSTKA, *horrified, walks backward in front of* MARKETA, *she walks behind him, they slowly circle the stage.*)

FOUSTKA: What are you doing here, for God's sake? Did you run away?

MARKETA: Tell him, please, when you see him, that all those things can't exist just for themselves, but that they must conceal some deeper design of existence, of the world, and of nature willing you . . .

FOUSTKA: Marketa, don't you recognize me? It's Henry . . .

MARKETA: Or could it be, perhaps, that the cosmos directly intended that one fine day it would see itself thus through our eyes and ask itself thus through our lips the very questions we're asking ourselves here and now?

FOUSTKA: You ought to go back—they'll help you—everything will be all right again—you'll see . . .

MARKETA (*singing*):
> How should I your true love know
> From another one?
> By his cockle hat and staff,
> And his sandal shoon.

(MARKETA *vanishes to the right. Offstage the sound of her singing can still be heard, gradually fading away.* FOUSTKA, *upset, crosses over to the table, quickly pours himself a drink, downs it in one gulp, and pours himself another. The* DIRECTOR *and* KOTRLY, *who have in the interim left the dance floor, appear at the right, holding hands. They pay no attention to* FOUSTKA *but are absorbed in their conversation.*)

DIRECTOR: Surely he tried to dance with you at the very least . . .

KOTRLY: Please stop it! Can't you talk about anything more interesting?

DIRECTOR: Did he try or not?

KOTRLY: All right, he did, if you really must know, then he did! But I won't tell you another thing.

(*The* DIRECTOR *and* KOTRLY *slowly cross the stage and head for the exit at left.*)

FOUSTKA: Excuse me, Sir . . .

(*The* DIRECTOR *and* KOTRLY *stop.*)

DIRECTOR: What do you want, Foustka?

(*Just then a cry of pain is heard from behind the bench.*)

NEUWIRTH (*offstage*): Ow!

(*The* DIRECTOR, KOTRLY, *and* FOUSTKA *look towards the bench with surprise. Out of the bushes emerges* NEUWIRTH, *holding his ear, obviously wounded. He is groaning.*)

94

KOTRLY: What in the world happened to you, Louie?

NEUWIRTH: Oh, nothing.

DIRECTOR: Is something the matter with your ear?

(NEUWIRTH *nods.*)

KOTRLY: Did something bite you?

(NEUWIRTH *nods, and with his head indicates the bushes from which he had just emerged and out of which now emerges an embarrassed* PETRUSHKA. *She is nervously straightening her hair and her costume. The* DIRECTOR *and* KOTRLY *grin and exchange knowing looks.* NEUWIRTH, *groaning and holding his ear, drags himself off to the right and disappears.* PETRUSHKA *timidly crosses the stage to the table and with shaking hands pours herself a small drink, which she swiftly drinks. The* DIRECTOR *and* KOTRLY *try to leave.*)

FOUSTKA: Excuse me, Sir . . .

DIRECTOR: What do you want, Foustka?

(*Just then the* DEPUTY *enters from the left. At first he doesn't see* PETRUSHKA, *who is hidden by* FOUSTKA.)

DEPUTY: Have you seen Petrushka?

(PETRUSHKA *goes up to the* DEPUTY, *smiles at him, and takes his hand; from this moment on they will hold hands as before.*)

Where were you, sweetie pie?

(PETRUSHKA *whispers something to the* DEPUTY, *he listens carefully, finally he nods in satisfaction. The* DIRECTOR *and* KOTRLY *try to leave.*)

FOUSTKA: Excuse me, Sir . . .

DIRECTOR: What do you want, Foustka?

FOUSTKA: I realize that you have a lot of other things on your mind right now, but on the other hand . . . having learned my lesson by what happened before . . I wouldn't want to neglect anything . . . You see, I have some new findings . . . I've even written them down on a piece of paper . . .

(FOUSTKA *begins to search, obviously looking for the paper. The* DIRECTOR *and the* DEPUTY *exchange knowing glances and then take a few steps forward, the one leading* KOTRLY *by the hand, the other,* PETRUSHKA, *and move to the center of the stage, where all four automatically form a sort of semicircle around* FOUSTKA. *A short pause.*)

DIRECTOR: Don't bother.

(FOUSTKA *looks at the* DIRECTOR *in surprise, then looks around at the others. A short, suspenseful pause.*)

FOUSTKA: I thought I . . .

(*Again, a suspenseful pause, which is finally interrupted by the* DIRECTOR.)

DIRECTOR (*sharply*): I'm not interested in what you thought, I'm not interested in your piece of paper, I'm not interested in you. The comedy, my dear Sir, is ended!

FOUSTKA: I don't understand—what comedy?

DIRECTOR: You greatly overestimated yourself and you greatly underestimated us, taking us for bigger idiots than we are.

DEPUTY: You still don't understand?

FOUSTKA: No.

DIRECTOR: Very well, then, I'll give it to you straight. We knew all along what you thought of us, we knew you were merely pretending to be loyal while hiding your real interests and ideas from us. But in spite of that we decided to give you a last chance. And so while seeming to believe that cock-and-bull story about your intention to work for us out in the field, we were curious to see how you would behave after having had your lesson and your supposed narrow escape, wondering whether you might not come to your senses after all. But instead, you took the hand we offered you and spat on it in a despicable way, thus definitively sealing your own fate.

FOUSTKA: That's not true!

DIRECTOR: You know perfectly well that it is!

FOUSTKA: Then prove it!

DIRECTOR (*to the* DEPUTY): Shall we oblige him?

DEPUTY: I'm in favor of it.

(*The* DIRECTOR *sharply whistles on his fingers. From the bower, where he had apparently been hidden for the entire scene,* FISTULA *leaps out.* FOUSTKA *is alarmed to see him.* FISTULA *quickly limps over to the* DIRECTOR.)

FISTULA: Did you call, Boss?

DIRECTOR: What did he tell you when you were at his house yesterday?

FISTULA: That he would pretend to be working as an informer for you, but in reality he, together with those you are fighting against, would use all their power to damage your information service. He literally said that he would be our—meaning their—man hidden in the heart of the enemy . . .

FOUSTKA (*screaming*): He's lying!

DIRECTOR: What did you say? Would you repeat that?

97

FOUSTKA: I said he's lying.

DIRECTOR: Man, you really have some nerve! How dare you accuse my close and faithful friend of many years and one of our best external agents of lying! Fistula never lies to us!

DEPUTY: That's precisely what I wanted to say, Sir! Fistula never lies to us!

(LORENCOVA *and the* SECRET MESSENGER *appear from the left, while at the same time the* LOVERS *appear from the right, all of whom have, in the interim, left the dance floor. Both pairs are holding hands. They join the others in such a way that the semicircle in the center of which* FOUSTKA *is standing unobtrusively widens at both sides in order to incorporate them.*)

FOUSTKA: So Fistula was an informer after all, and you planted him on me to test me! What an imbecile I was not to throw him out right away! Vilma, I apologize to you for my absurd suspicions that made me lose you! Mrs. Houbova, I apologize to you—of course you knew the truth right away.

DIRECTOR: Who's he talking to?

FISTULA: His landlady, Boss.

DIRECTOR: Naturally you're not the only person in the world I'm interested in. I test everybody—you'd be surprised how long it sometimes takes, compared to your trivial case—for me to get at the truth, in one way or another!

FOUSTKA (*to* FISTULA): So I fell for your line after all!

FISTULA: I beg your pardon, Doctor Foustka. (*To the* DIRECTOR:) Is he still a doctor?

DIRECTOR: Who gives a shit?

FISTULA: I beg your pardon, Doctor Foustka, but there you go again, oversimplifying! Didn't I make it clear all along, by dropping hints and even spelling it out, that you had a number of alternatives, and that you alone were the master of your fate! You weren't a victim of my line, but of your own; or rather, of your pride, which made you think that you'd be able to play both ends against the middle and still get away with it! Or have you forgotten how carefully I explained to you that if a person doesn't want to come to a bad end, he must respect some form of authority, it almost doesn't matter which, and that even a revolution has its own laws? I don't see how I could have made things more obvious than that! My conscience is clear, I did what I could. Why, I couldn't have fulfilled my mission more correctly! The fact that you didn't understand anything, well, I'm afraid that's your tough luck.

DIRECTOR: Fistula is right, as ever. You cannot serve two masters at once and deceive them both at the same time! You cannot take from everyone and give nothing in return! You simply must take a side!

DEPUTY: That's precisely what I just wanted to say, Sir! You simply must take a side!

(The music grows noticeably louder. The tango that played earlier is heard again. At the same moment VILMA runs onstage from the left and the DANCER from the right, having in the interim left the dance floor. They run through the group of people to the center of the stage, where they fall into each other's arms and commence to do another complicated tango figure, during which the DANCER does a "dip" almost to the ground with VILMA. The music suddenly grows quiet, and VILMA and the DANCER, holding hands just as all the other couples in the room are doing, quietly join the semicircle.)

Foustka: It's paradoxical, but now that I've definitively lost and my knowledge serves no purpose to me, I'm finally beginning to understand it all! Fistula is right: I was an arrogant madman who thought he could exploit the devil without signing away his soul to him! But as everyone knows, one can't deceive the devil!

(Neuwirth, *with a large bandage on his ear, enters from the right, just as* Marketa *runs in from the left. When she sees* Neuwirth *she calls out to him.*)

Marketa: Papa!

(Marketa *runs up to* Neuwirth *and seizes his hand. He is a little embarrassed. And even they reluctantly become part of the semicircle.*)

Fistula: Wait a minute, now! Hold it! I never said that there is such a thing as a devil, not even while I was engaged in that provocation.

Foustka: But I'm saying it! And he's actually here among us!

Fistula: Are you referring to me?

Foustka: You're just a subordinate little fiend!

Director: I know your opinions, Foustka, and therefore I understand this metaphor of yours as well. Through me, you want to accuse modern science of being the true source of all evil. Isn't that right?

Foustka: No, it isn't! Through you, I want to accuse the pride of that intolerant, all-powerful, and self-serving power that uses the sciences merely as a handy weapon for shooting down anything that threatens it, that is, anything that doesn't derive its authority from this power or that is related to an authority deriving its powers elsewhere.

100

DIRECTOR: That's the legacy you wish to leave this world, Foustka?

FOUSTKA: Yes!

DIRECTOR: I find it a little banal. In countries without censorship every halfway clever little hack journalist churns out stuff like that these days! But a legacy is a legacy, so in spite of what you think of me, I'll give you an example of how tolerant I am by overlooking my reservations and applauding your last testament!

(The DIRECTOR begins to clap lightly, and all the others gradually join in. At the same time the music grows louder—it is hard, wild, and aggressive rock music, a variation of the music heard before the performance and during the pauses. The clapping soon becomes rhythmic, in time with the music, which grows ever louder, slowly becoming almost deafening. Everyone onstage, with the exception of FOUSTKA, gradually begins to move suggestively in time with the music. At first, while clapping, they begin to wriggle gently, swaying and shaking to the music. Then this movement slowly changes into dancing. At first they each dance alone, then in couples, and finally all together. The dance is ever wilder, until it becomes a crazy, orgiastic masked ball or witches' sabbath. FOUSTKA does not participate but wanders around in confusion, weaving in and out among the dancers, who variously bump into him, so that he completely loses his sense of direction and is unable to escape, though he would clearly like to. KOTRLY, who slipped away from the witches' sabbath earlier, now returns, carrying a bowl with flames playing at the surface. He twists in and out among the dancers with it, trying to get to the bower, where he finally succeeds in putting the bowl down. However, on the way there he also manages to ignite Foustka's cape, so that a new chaotic element is added to the witches' sabbath in the person of the burning FOUSTKA, who now, completely panicked, races around the stage.)

Shortly thereafter everyone is surrounded by a thick cloud of smoke streaming in from the bower where KOTRLY *has placed his bowl. The music blasts away. Nothing can be seen onstage. Smoke penetrates the audience. Then the music suddenly stops, the house lights go on, the smoke fades, and it becomes evident that at some point during all this the curtain has fallen. After a very brief silence, music comes on again, now at a bearable level of loudness—the most banal commercial music possible. If the smoke—or the play itself—hasn't caused the audience to flee, and if there are still a few left in the audience who might even want to applaud, let the first to take a bow and thank the audience be a fireman in full uniform with a helmet on his head and a fire extinguisher in his hand.)*